# HIDDEN HISTORY
## *of*
## LEWES

# HIDDEN
# HISTORY
## *of*
# LEWES

*Michael Morgan*

THE
History
PRESS

Published by The History Press
Charleston, SC 29403
www.historypress.net

First published 2014

Manufactured in the United States

ISBN 978.1.62619.064.1

Library of Congress CIP data applied for.

# CONTENTS

# CONTENTS

# PREFACE

E ach year, thousands of visitors to Lewes stroll the town's picturesque streets, tour the buildings of the Lewes Historical Society and enjoy the view from Memorial Park. There is much to see, but there is also much that is hidden. Lost beneath the old buildings and the drifting sands lie the specters of the Native American shell mounds, the original Dutch settlement, the utopian colony of Pieter Cornelisz Plockhoy and a host of other episodes in the town's history. This book is an attempt to resurrect many of the events and details from better-known chapters in the history of Lewes and indicate some of the locations where they may be seen.

I would like to thank the countless people who provided assistance in answering my questions and securing images for this book, especially Chuck Fithian, curator of Archaeology for the State of Delaware's Historical and Cultural Affairs; Dan Griffith of the Archaeological Society of Delaware; Jim Hall and George Contant at the Delaware State Parks Cultural Resources Unit; Bridget Warner, site supervisor of the Zwaanendael Museum; Mchael DiPaolo, executive director of the Lewes Historical Society; and Randy L. Goss, coordinator of Accessing and Processing/Photo Archivist/Preservation officer at the Delaware Public Archives. I would also like to thank my son, Tom, and his wife, Karla, for their support and technical assistance. Finally, I would like to thank my wife, Madelyn, for her constant editorial advice and support. She read every word in this book numerous times and spent countless hours correcting my spelling, punctuation and grammar. Without her help and support, this book would not have been possible.

A replica of the East End Lighthouse on Route 9 welcomes visitors to Lewes. *Photo by Michael Morgan.*

# Chapter 1

# DOWN PILOTTOWN ROAD

## HE THAT WILL THOROUGHLY DISCOVER THIS GREAT BAY

When Henry Hudson guided the *Half Moon* around the smooth arch of Cape Henlopen and into Delaware Bay in August 1609, the veteran English mariner was sailing for Dutch employers. Hudson was searching for a water route to the Pacific, but he was quickly convinced that this shoaly bay did not lead across the continent. After a brief stay, Hudson sailed back into the Atlantic. The log of the *Half Moon* warned, "And he that will thoroughly discover this great bay, must have a small pinnace, that must draw but four or five foot water, to sound before him."

If any of the Siconese living near the cape had spotted Hudson's ship, they would not have been surprised. Large European ships had sailed along the Atlantic Coast on several occasions. The Siconese were part of the Algonquian language group of American Indians who inhabited the area from the Delmarva Peninsula to the Hudson River. These Native Americans, who are sometimes grouped together as the Lenape, lived in various tribal groups, but the delineation of these tribes was sometimes unclear. During planting time in the spring and early summer and when it came time to harvest their crops, the Siconese lived in established towns, at least one of which was near the cape that marked the southern entrance to the bay.

The homes of the Siconese, known as wigwams, were made from bark laid on a wicker frame with reed mats covering the floor. Some of these structures were small, domelike buildings, and others were more rectangular. Around the wigwams, the Native Americans planted corn, beans, pumpkins and squash. They also picked wild berries, gathered nuts and dug roots to supplement their diets.

The Siconese left their permanent homes during the winter to hunt in the game-filled forests of southern Delaware. The deer and smaller animals that they killed provided food, and the animal skins provided clothing. When the Siconese were threatened by other tribes, the women and children accompanied the men on the winter hunts. The winter hunts were only temporary excursions; the Siconese were otherwise at home by the Delaware Bay that teemed with fish, crabs, oysters and an occasional whale. They would leave their wigwams, which were on the high ground southwest of the creek, and use dugout canoes to reach the beaches of the cape, where they feasted on oysters on the beach; their discarded shells accumulated into large mounds, some measuring thirty feet high and one hundred feet in diameter. Bleached by the sun, they gleamed like the alabaster covering of an ancient temple. Farther back from the beach stood the great dune, a one-hundred-foot-high mountain of sand covered by a forest of pine trees.

The Siconese established trails that led southward along the coast toward Assateague and northward inland toward Pennsylvania. They traded with other tribes for things that they did not have. Travel was on foot or by dugout canoes, vessels that could be paddled up the shallow rivers of Delaware and portaged over to the rivers that emptied into Chesapeake Bay. It may have been on one of these trading expeditions that the Siconese first learned of the fair-skinned visitors who came from the sea.

In 1492, when Christopher Columbus completed his initial voyage across the Atlantic, he unleashed a flood of Spanish explorers who sailed the area around the Caribbean Sea. At the same time, English and French adventurers explored Newfoundland and the St. Lawrence River, and reports of these visitors with their large ships, metal suits and astonishing horses may have reached the Siconese. In 1524, Giovanni da Verrazano, an Italian explorer sailing for France, passed the Delmarva coast, and it might be possible that the Siconese saw his ship; however, it is not likely because Verrazano sailed so far off the coast that he missed the entrance to Delaware Bay. More likely, the Siconese caught a glimpse of Pedro de Quejo, a Spanish adventurer who is believed to have entered the Delaware and sailed along the bay's western shore. The Siconese may also have learned of the "Lost Colony" that the English planted on Roanoke Island in the 1580s. Word of the Jamestown colony that was established by the English in 1607 could have filtered up to the Siconese, but the Native Americans on Lewes Creek surely heard reports of Captain John Smith's 1608 voyage up the Nanticoke River, where the Native Americans welcomed the English captain from Jamestown with a shower of arrows that forced Smith to anchor in the middle of the river. Alerted by Smith's encounter with the Native Americans, the Siconese would not have been surprised the next year when Henry Hudson sailed the *Half Moon* around Cape Henlopen into Delaware Bay, which the Dutch called "South River."

Four years after Hudson entered Delaware Bay, the Dutch explorer Adrian Block landed on Manhattan Island, where his ship was destroyed by fire. With the help of Native American inhabitants of Manhattan, Block built shelters for his crew, and using newly cut timber and fittings salvaged from his burnt ship, Block constructed a small vessel that he named the *Onrust*, Dutch for "Restless."

The *Onrust* was just over forty-four feet long and less than twelve feet wide,

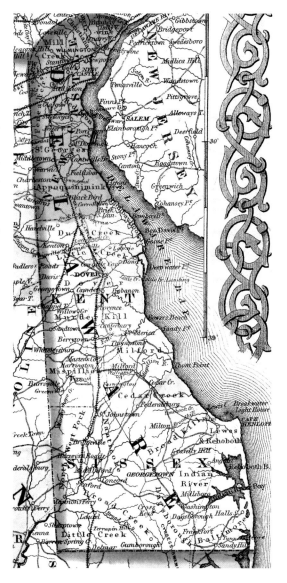

This nineteenth-century map shows the location of Cape Henlopen and Lewes at the mouth of Delaware Bay. *Courtesy of the Delaware Public Archives.*

and it drew only a few feet of water. This small vessel was ideal to explore Delaware Bay. Block called the *Onrust* a "Yacht," a small vessel that could scurry between the larger ships of a fleet. In the spring of 1614, Block explored Long Island Sound and the southern New England coast. Block Island, off the Rhode Island coast, was named after this resourceful explorer.

When Block encountered a Dutch ship, he decided to return to Europe, and he turned the command of the *Onrust* over to Captain Cornelius Hendrickson, who sailed the *Onrust* southward until he reached the mouth of Delaware Bay. Unlike Henry Hudson, who was afraid of running aground on a shoal in the *Half Moon*, Hendrickson's *Onrust*, with its shallow draft, enabled him to navigate the Delaware's dangerous waters. After getting a thorough examination of the western shore of the bay, Hendrickson encountered a larger Dutch ship and returned to Holland.

Back in Europe, Hendrickson received little recognition for his exploration of Delaware Bay. His reports of the natural resources of the bay area, however, helped initiate an interest in the Mid-Atlantic Coast, and in 1620, Captain Cornelius Jacobsen Mey arrived at the mouth of Delaware Bay aboard the *Blijde Bootschap*, "Glad Tidings." Mey successfully navigated the Delaware's many shoals and shallows, and a few years later, he helped to establish the first European settlement on the Delaware River at Fort Nassau in New Jersey.

As was the custom when captains charted unfamiliar waters, Mey attached names to prominent geographic features. He called the bay "Nieuw Port Mey," and he christened the promontory on the northern side of the estuary's entrance "Cape Mey." After the Dutch captain named the sandy cape on the bay's southern shore "Cape Cornelius," Mey left the bay and sailed southward for about twenty miles, where Mey noticed a slight bulge in the coast at Fenwick Island. He concluded that he was passing a cape. The Dutch captain dubbed the protrusion in the coastline "Cape Henlopen," and with this done, Mey ended his naming efforts and sailed home.

Cape Mey would be corrupted into Cape May, and Nieuw Port Mey never became a popular name for the Delaware Bay. The designation of Fenwick Island as Cape Henlopen did not last, and the name gravitated northward to denote the cape at the southern entrance of the great bay where the Siconese made their homes. Whether or not Mey was the first European to initiate contact with the Siconese, the Native Americans became used to seeing the European ships in the bay, and in 1629, a group of Dutchmen stopped at Lewes Creek to meet with the Siconese.

When the Dutch West India Company authorized the establishment of colonies in America, a group led by Samuel Godyn, Kiliaen Van Rensselaer and Sameul Bloomaert decided to plant a colony in the Cape Henlopen area as a whaling station and farming area. They dispatched Gillis Houset to America, and he met with the leaders of the Siconese. On June 1, 1629, the Dutch presented cloth, iron tools and other items to the Siconese, who in turn made their mark on a document that ceded the land to the Dutch. The idea of purchasing land was foreign to the Native Americans, who probably believed that they were signing a use agreement. As long as the Dutch continued to show their friendship, they were free to use the land. The way was clear for a Dutch settlement near Lewes Creek. For the time being, the shell mounds along the beach still glimmered brightly, but the arrival of the Europeans was the beginning of the end of the Siconese's way of life.

## SKULLS AND BONES OF OUR PEOPLE

After Captain Peter Heyes edged the *Walvis* around Cape Henlopen in 1631, he steered the small sailing ship toward shore. It had been two years since the Dutch had "purchased" the land near the cape from the Siconese. Aboard the ship, several dozen Dutch colonists got their first glimpse of the gleaming shell mounds of the Siconese, the dense pine forest and the towering dunes of the cape. As the *Walvis* entered Delaware Bay, Heyes steered for the languid waters of the Whorekill, so named, a colonist explained several years later, because "[the Dutch] traded with the Indians and frequent[ed] so much with the Indian women till they got…the pox and so they named that place the Whorekill [Lewes Creek]." The word *kill* means "creek" or "river" in Dutch. The name "Whorekill" would also be applied to the area that the Dutch occupied along the banks of Delaware Bay. After enduring weeks of cramped quarters aboard the *Walvis*, the apparently empty and endless landscape was a welcome sight for the settlers, who were eager to stretch their legs on dry land. Heyes expertly guided the ship into the mouth of the Whorekill, and a short time later, the colonists scrambled ashore.

Having landed in an unfamiliar and foreign world, the Dutch settlers did what every other group of Europeans did when they established a new colony: they built a fort. During the seventeenth century, competing nations were forever on the verge of war. The next sail that appeared on the horizon might belong to an enemy warship. A low bluff opposite the mouth of the Whorekill provided a firm and level foundation for the modest fortification, and the Dutch colonists set about felling trees and splitting logs into planks.

A replica of the *Kalmar Nyckel*, which brought the first Swedish colonists to the Wilmington area, sails past the Delaware Breakwater. The Dutch colonists at Swanendael arrived in similar ships. *Photo by Michael Morgan.*

As the colonists worked, the outline of a square-shaped fort began to appear. The northern corner of the fort pointed directly toward the mouth of the Whorekill. Protruding from the northern corner, a triangular-shaped bastion was erected by the Dutch colonists. In most forts, bastions had raised floors on which cannons could be mounted. In addition to the bastion at the northern corner of the fort, settlers erected a similar structure at the southern corner. Defenders stationed in the bastions had a clear field of fire along each of the fort's four walls. The colonists were confident that their fort would enable them to defend the new colony, which they dubbed *Swanendael*, or "Valley of the Swans." Many years later, it became fashionable to call the Dutch settlement along the Whorekill "Zwaanendael," but that name does not appear in colonial documents.

The Swanendael settlers arrived at Cape Henlopen during the golden age of Dutch power, when Dutch ships carried European goods to far-flung ports, Dutch banks handled a major share of Europe's money and Dutch artists, such as Rembrandt and Vermeer, painted some of Europe's greatest masterpieces. Baruch Spinoza and René Descartes were among Europe's leading thinkers, and Antony van Leeuwenhoek made startling discoveries

Conjectural drawing of the Swanendael settlement. *Drawing by Madelyn Morgan.*

This early twentieth-century photo shows the bluff on Pilottown Road, where it is believed that the Swanendael settlement stood. *Courtesy of the Delaware Public Archives.*

in science. It was a time when mania for tulips broke out and the demand for bulbs sent prices skyrocketing until a single bulb could be worth as much as an average person could earn in a year.

15

The Netherlands shared with England a common loathing of Catholic Spain, a love of their Protestant religion and a vigorous seafaring heritage. David de Vries was just one of the many Dutch entrepreneurs who helped establish colonies in Asia, Africa and America. Born in La Rachelle, France,

David de Vries, a veteran mariner, was a leader of the company that established Swanendael, but he was not among the colony's first settlers. *Courtesy of the Delaware Public Archives.*

in the last decade of the sixteenth century, de Vries moved to Holland with his family when he was still very young. By the time he was twenty years old, de Vries commanded a ship engaged in the Mediterranean trade. He made his first Atlantic crossing in 1620, the year that the Pilgrims, who had spent time in Holland, landed at Plymouth Rock. Not all of his voyages were peaceful, but de Vries was able to survive fierce ocean storms and attacks by bloodthirsty pirates.

De Vries was a leader of the Swanendael colony, but he did not accompany the initial group of colonists. In 1632, as de Vries prepared an expedition to the settlement on the Whorekill, he became discouraged when reports reached the Netherlands that the first colonists had failed to find many whales in Delaware, and he considered abandoning the project. Other Dutch entrepreneurs were more optimistic. According to de Vries, "It was therefore again resolved to undertake a voyage for the whale fishery, and that I myself should go as patron, and as commander of the ship and yacht, and should endeavor to be there in December in order to conduct the whale fishing during the winter, as the whales come in the winter and remain till March."

Before de Vries left the Netherlands, he received another unsettling report about Swanendael. The palisade stockade had been destroyed, and all of the colonists had been killed. On December 2, 1632, de Vries arrived off the coast of Delaware, and he noticed that the land, "gave a sweet perfume, as the wind came from the north-west, which blew off the land, and caused these sweet odors." When de Vries sailed into the Delaware, he recalled in his memoirs, "Sailed into the south bay…and saw immediately a whale near the ship. [I knew] that this would be royal work—the whales so numerous—and the land so fine for cultivation."

Unfortunately, de Vries's euphoria was crushed when he reached the Whorekill and spotted the charred remains of the fort at Swanendael, where, "coming by our house [fort] which was destroyed, [we] found it well beset with palisades in place of breastworks, but it was almost burnt up. Found lying here and there the skulls and bones of our people and the heads of the horses and cows which they had brought with them."

A few days later, a Native American showed de Vries the place where the Swanendael settlers had set up a pole to which they attached a piece of tin painted with the coat of arms of Holland. The Native American told de Vries that one of the Siconese had innocently taken the tin to make a pipe for tobacco, upsetting the Dutch settlers. When the colonists complained to the Siconese, the Native American said, "They went away and slew the chief who had done it and brought a token of the dead to the house to those in command, who told them that they wished they had not done it, that they should have brought him to them, as they wished to have forbidden him not to [do] the like again."

After this scolding from the Dutch colonists, the incident further escalated. The Native American told de Vries, "They then went away, and the friends of the murdered chief incited their friends…to set about the work of revenge."

A few days later, several Siconese arrived at Swanendael with a number of beaver skins to trade with the Dutch settlers. Having gained entrance to the fort, the disgruntled Native Americans attacked and killed all the settlers of Swanendael.

Some historians have cast doubt on this story. A petty theft would usually result in an offer of gifts to make amends to the offended party rather than the summary execution of the Siconese who took the Dutch sign. However it happened, the relationship between Native Americans and the settlers of Swanendael deteriorated after the colonists established the first settlement in Delaware, which resulted in the death of all thirty-two European colonists.

When de Vries and the other Dutch leaders abandoned the Whorekill, they left behind the scorched timbers of Swanendael to decay amid the "sweet perfume" of the Delaware countryside. A decade after the failure of the Swanendael colony, de Vries returned to America and settled on the New Jersey side of the Hudson River, across from Manhattan Island. His new settlement was named *Vriessendael*, or "de Vries's Valley." In 1643, an altercation over a missing beaver coat led to the killing of two colonists. De Vries saw immediately that the situation was similar to what had happened at Swanendael and that theft could quickly escalate into violence.

By 1643, there were scores of Dutch colonists living on the lower Hudson River, and it was the colonists who organized an armed expedition against the unsuspecting Native Americans. Knowing what happened in Delaware, de Vries pleaded with the colonial leaders to cancel the attack but to no avail. During the night, Dutch colonists attacked a Native American village at Pavonia while the Indians were still asleep, and eighty men, women and children were slaughtered. The massacre at Pavonia led to reprisals by the Native Americans, and among the settlements to be destroyed was Vriessendael. Fortunately, de Vries survived the attacks, and shortly afterward, he returned to Europe with the memory of "the skulls and bones of our people" lying in the field around the charred remains of Swanendael seared into his mind.

# To a Nail

Three decades after the destruction of Swanendael, Pieter Cornelisz Plockhoy stepped ashore at the Whorekill. Not much had changed since de Vries abandoned the colony near Cape Henlopen. Although the Siconese's numbers may have decreased, they still lived in wigwams, fished in Delaware Bay and threw oyster shells onto mounds that lined the beach. Following the failure of Swanendael, the Dutch continued to maintain their settlements on the New Jersey side of the Delaware, and an occasional English ship sailed past Cape Henlopen.

In 1629, one of those English ships carried George Calvert, the first Lord Baltimore, from his Avalon colony in Newfoundland to Jamestown, Virginia. Calvert, a former member of the Privy Council, liked what he saw in the Chesapeake area. When he returned to England, Calvert applied for a grant for a new colony to the north of Virginia that would include "that Part of the Bay of Delaware on the North, which lieth under the Fortieth Degree of North Latitude…in a country hitherto uncultivated." The fortieth parallel was in the vicinity of Philadelphia and, in effect, Calvert's grant included all of Delaware.

George Calvert died in 1632, and King Charles I granted Maryland to George's son Cecil, second Lord Baltimore. Two years later, the first Maryland colonists arrived on a tributary of the Potomac River. Initially, the second Lord Baltimore and the Maryland colonists focused on establishment of settlements near Chesapeake Bay, but eventually, they would cast jealous eyes on land bordering Delaware Bay. Unfortunately for Baltimore, the Swanendael colonists cultivated the land around Cape Henlopen the year before he received his grant.

While Lord Baltimore and the Marylanders were busy setting up their colony and scheming to maintain their claim to the land on "that Part of the Bay of Delaware on the North…under the Fortieth Degree of North Latitude," Sweden established a colony at the future site of Wilmington. The arrival of the Swedes in 1638 would pit Sweden against the Netherlands over their settlements on the Delaware; eventually, the Dutch ousted the Swedes, and a consolidated New Netherlands stretched from the Delaware Bay across New Jersey to Manhattan Island and up the Hudson River. The English did not take lightly to the growing power of the Dutch in North America.

During the first half of the seventeenth century, Europe was embroiled in a variety of religious, economic and territorial conflicts that pitted Protestant against Catholic, rich against poor and a host of European countries against one another. The Thirty Years War from 1618 to 1648 was one of the most destructive that Europe had ever endured. The English Revolution led to the execution of Charles I, the rise of the Puritans under Oliver Cromwell and the return of the monarchy all happening from 1642 to 1660. Out of this chaos came those who dreamt of a world where there would be no lords, no servants and no religious strife. Such was the dream of Pieter Plockhoy, and he was determined to bring that dream to reality.

Although not much is known of his early life, it is believed that Plockhoy was from Zierikzee in the Zeeland province of Holland. In 1658, he went to England to secure financing for an egalitarian colony that Plockhoy wished to establish in America. In his colony, there would be no social classes, "no lordship or servile slavery." The settlement was to be founded "upon righteousness, upon love and upon brotherly union. Religious diversity was to be permitted as long as "brotherhood and unity possess them all."

Despite the lofty ideals of his project, Plockhoy was unable to obtain backing in England, and he returned to the Netherlands. After several years of effort, he was able to convince the City of Amsterdam to support his settlement. The Dutch dreamer set about recruiting colonists who would "work at farming, fishing, handicraft, etc." He was able to convince forty-one settlers to join him, and in May 1663, Plockhoy and his followers set sail on the *St. Jacob*.

In July, the *St. Jacob* arrived off Cape Henlopen, and Plockhoy led the colonists and "their baggage and farm utensils" ashore. Sometime before Plockhoy and his followers arrived at the Whorekill, the Dutch had erected a small military outpost, but there were still very few Europeans living in the Cape Henlopen area. Plockhoy's forty-one settlers outnumbered those at the Swanendael settlement, and they would have had a substantial impact on the Cape Henlopen area.

Plockhoy may have dreamt of a world in which all people and all nations would live in harmony, but that was not the reality seventeenth century world. The English and the Dutch were competitors for colonies around the world, and the relationship between the two countries degenerated into war. A little more than one year after Plockhoy established his settlement near Cape Henlopen, the British targeted the Dutch colonies in North America for conquest. After Peter Stuyvesant surrendered the Dutch colony on Manhattan Island, the English dispatched Sir Robert Carr to Delaware, where he had little difficulty capturing Plockhoy's settlement, and he boasted that he destroyed the "quaking society of Plockhoy to a nail."

This oft-repeated but unsubstantiated claim became the final word on the idealistic Whorekill settlement. According to some sources, many, but not all, of Plockhoy's followers were taken to Virginia, where they were sold as servants. It is not known whether Plockhoy survived Carr's attack, but if he did, he probably died a short time later.

Some writers have praised Plockhoy for being an early voice against slavery and for being a pioneer of social and political democracy, but his noble experiment had little effect on the Dutch settlement at the Whorekill. Only a few Europeans remained in the Cape Henlopen area, and the time was ripe for Lord Baltimore and the Marylanders to press their claims to the land along the Whorekill.

## He Must Burn All Their Houses

Helmanus Wiltbank may have been a contemporary of Pieter Plockhoy, or he may have arrived at the Whorekill after Plockhoy's settlement was destroyed. According to tradition, Wiltbank's ship foundered near Cape Henlopen, and the intrepid colonist, along with his wife and children, swam ashore. Whenever he arrived, Wiltbank became one of the leaders of the small cluster of European colonists living on the Whorekill.

In 1671, Wiltbank took a census of the settlers living along the southern shores of Delaware Bay. Only the names of the adult men were listed, but Wiltbank's census indicated whether their wives were living with them and the number of the children they had. Wiltbank, Alexander Molestine, Ottho Wolgast, James Weeden, John Roades and Daniel Brun all had their wives with them. The Wiltbank, Molestine and Weeden families had two children each. The Wolgast family had a son, and the Roades family had three sons and two daughters. Four of these families had servants. William Klasen is recorded with "two daughters, [and] one child," who may have been an infant. Wiltbank did not list Klasen's wife, and she may have died in childbirth. Daniel Brun and his wife were childless, and John Collison, Brun's business partner, lived with him. There were eight single men: Jan Michiels, brothers Anthony and Abraham Pieters, Pieter Hanaz, Pieter Gromendick, Anthany Hansen, Herman Cornlissen and Hendrick Drochstraaeten. The total was forty-seven colonists.

The Wiltbank and the Molestine families, in addition to the Pieters brothers, owned rectangular parcels of land that stretched from the

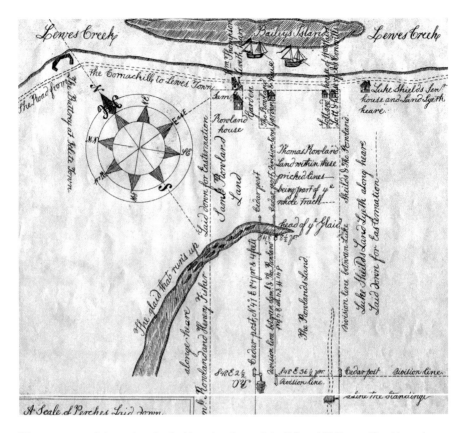

The remnants of the early colonists' lots that fronted the Whorekill (Lewes Creek) can be seen this eighteenth-century map. *Courtesy of the Delaware Public Archives.*

Whorekill for a mile to the marshland along Pagan Creek. Averaging over one hundred acres apiece, these parcels were designed for farming. The short side of these parcels, however, provided one thousand feet of frontage on the Whorekill, where owners of these lots could build docks to ship the yield from their farms. Where the rest of the inhabitants listed by Wiltbank lived has not been determined, but many of them might have lived on smaller plots that were bunched together east of Wiltbank's farm. Not all the families Wiltbank listed lived near the creek, as John Roades and his family lived several miles from Cape Henlopen. Wiltbank took his census in May 1671, and a month later, Thomas Jones made his first visit to the area.

When the conflict between Great Britain and the Netherlands entered a temporary lull, Lord Baltimore saw an opportunity to press his claims to "that Part of the Bay of Delaware on the North, which lieth under the

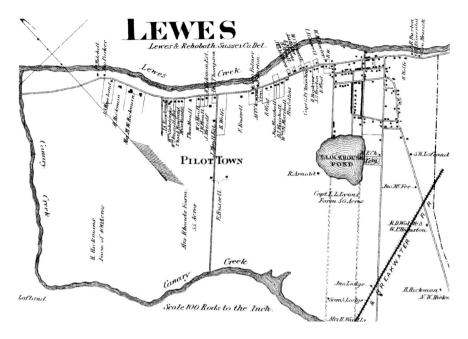

On this nineteenth-century map, the early settlements are to the left and the town of Lewes is to the right. *Courtesy of the Delaware Public Archives.*

Fortieth Degree of North Latitude." In June 1671, Captain Thomas Jones with a half dozen armed horsemen arrived at the homes of Wiltbank and his neighbors and tied them up. With the residents of the Whorekill held captive in their own homes, the Marylanders were free to pillage the town.

Jones left the Whorekill with his booty, but he returned in September with thirty horsemen and again plundered the residents of the Whorekill of their valuables. In addition, Jones demanded that the Dutch colonists sign an oath of allegiance to Lord Baltimore.

Apparently, the Maryland authorities were not satisfied with the forced oaths of allegiance given by the Whorekill settlers. In 1673, Governor Charles Calvert (son of Lord Baltimore) complained that Dutch settlers had taken possession of the area around Cape Henlopen "by force of arms to the utter ruin of several inhabitants of the said county and the dishonor of the said Lord of his just rights."

On November 17, Calvert issued a commission to Captain Thomas Howell to assemble forty armed men, who were to be "sufficiently provide with arms and ammunition and…to [be] trained…in the art of war." After his small army was ready, Howell was to lead them to the coast to establish control over the settlements around Cape Henlopen. If the Delaware colonists resisted, Howell was "to fight and overcome, kill, destroy, and vanquish as occasion shall require." Calvert went on to comment, "And if it shall so happen (as I do not in the least doubt) that you shall win the said place by assault, surprise."

In December, Howell led his armed band of Marylanders toward the Whorekill; and when they approached the settlement near Cape Henlopen, the Marylanders drew their swords. The Dutch settlers did not resist, and Howell began a protracted occupation of the budding town. The Marylanders spent several weeks in the Whorekill idling away their time by killing the colonists' livestock and ransacking the Dutch settlers' homes. When Harmon Conellison (who had a commission from Lord Baltimore to trade with the Native Americans and settlers of Maryland) refused to say where his beaver and other fur pelts were stored, Howell held a burning match to Conellison's finger until he disclosed their whereabouts.

By the third week of December, Howell called on the colonists to assemble with their weapons and ammunition on the pretext that they were going to do some sort of militia drill. Howell then, "caused all inhabitants of the county or province to be warned to come to Whorekill Town to muster with order[s] to bring all their arms and ammunition." When the Whorekill residents complied with this request, Howell disarmed them and announced, "That he must tell them with grief that his orders from the Lord Baltimore was that he must burn all their houses and that he must not leave one stick standing."

The Marylanders spread through the settlement and began to set fire to the buildings. Several pregnant women went to Howell and begged him to spare one building so that they could survive the coming winter. The Maryland commander answered, "I must observe my orders. I cannot spare any buildings." Howell went on to say, "If God spared you one, you can have it."

When Howell's men reached Alexander Moulston's farm near the inlet, they immediately set fire to several structures that were near a thatch barn. As the flames licked through the buildings, a shower of sparks began to rain down on the thatch barn; and it seemed only a matter of time before it, too, burst into flames. Captain Howell, however, declared, "If that thatched barn does not burn, it will be safe."

Three times the embers from other buildings set fire to the thatched barn; and each time, the fire went out. Seeing this, Howell said that "God has saved this thatch barn and I dare not meddle anymore." The Marylanders let the divinely protected barn stand, but the rest of the Whorekill buildings were consumed by the flames. Richard Patte had a house and two storehouses full of tobacco and corn. Patte, who had a wife and several small children, asked Howell for permission to build a small thatch shed or cabin to shelter his family. Howell answered that "it was death to build anything," and Patte replied, "Then knock them on the head and end their days." The unsympathetic Howell answered, "My commission did not reach that far."

In addition to burning the homes near the creek, Howell's men scoured the countryside looking for colonists who had not settled near Cape Henlopen. The Marylanders arrived at the farm of John Roades. It consisted of a dwelling house, a seventy-foot-long tobacco house, a milk house and other outbuildings. Again, the Marylanders gave the Roades family fifteen minutes to gather their valuables before they set fire to the house by carrying flaming wheat sheaves into the rooms of the dwelling to hasten the fire.

Having put all of the Dutch buildings in the Whorekill to the torch, Howell's party reassembled near the creek. They loaded their loot, which included arms, ammunition and even small boats and left the smoldering remains of the Whorekill. According to Wiltbank, "They burned and marched away and left us in unbearable conditions, so that all ye inhabitants (except a few) were forced to leave the place for want of provisions and [those who] were left in [the] place could not go because their wives were big with child." Some of residents of Whorekill attempted to reach New York and other places. Sadly, it was reported that "two were murdered, namely John Roades, Sr., and Thomas Tilley by the Indians."

The people of the Whorekill had suffered the "barbarous cruelty of ye Lord Baltimore," but they immediately set to work salvaging whatever they could from their burnt buildings. The next day, some may have momentarily paused to recall that it was Christmas Day.

## When You Go

Near the end of Pilottown Road overlooking the inlet, there is a modest stone monument that commemorates the founding of the ill-fated Swanendael colony. The chiseled inscription reads, "Erected by the state of Delaware to commemorate the settlement on this spot, of the first Dutch colony under de Vries. A.D. 1631. Here was the cradling of a state." When the monument was erected in the early twentieth century, the stone sat atop of a barren bluff near the southwestern bank of Lewes Creek. The natural attraction of this high ground was so enduring that the Siconese, European settlers

The monument dedicated to the memory of the Swanendael settlement was surrounded by barren ground when it was first erected in 1909. *Courtesy of the Delaware Public Archives.*

The first boat going through the newly dredged and stabilized inlet in 1937. *Courtesy of the Delaware Public Archives.*

and twentieth-century homeowners used it for their homes. The monument is now encircled by evergreen trees and bushes, the creek has been filled with modern pleasure boats and the inlet, which once was a meandering waterway, has been stabilized.

The memorial cross in St. Peter's Cemetery across Pilottown Road from the monument to the Swanendael settlement. *Photo by Michael Morgan.*

Across Pilottown Road is St. Peter's Cemetery, created when the yard surrounding the church became too crowded to accommodate the earthly remains of the faithful. There is speculation that the cemetery sits on the site of the Swanendael settlement, and in 1981, a stone cross was erected to commemorate the three hundredth anniversary of the grant of land to the Lewes Anglican congregation and in memory of the "first settlers who died here in 1631." Although there have been several archaeological attempts to locate the remains of the Swanendael settlement, the results have been inconclusive. For now, the remains of the Siconese wigwams, original Dutch settlement, Plockhoy's egalitarian colony and the homes burned by the Marylanders are buried beneath the homes and manicured lawns along Pilottown Road.

# Chapter 2

# ON THE BANKS OF
# THE WHOREKILL

## FOOLS, KNAVES AND ROGUES

Seven years after Howell's destructive raid, several families who survived the attack were still living in the Whorekill, including the Wiltbank, Molestine, Wolgast and Roades families. Plockhoy's blind son, Cornelisz, was not included in Wiltbank's 1671 census, but he survived Carr's raid and the burning of the town by Thomas Howell and was living on the banks of the Whorekill in 1678.

In February 1674, the Treaty of Westminster transferred the Dutch lands in North America permanently to the English. Charles II of England generously gave the lands that had composed New Netherland, including the lands along Delaware Bay, to his brother James, the Duke of York. With England firmly in control of the lands along the Delaware, the way was clear for more colonists to settle in the Whorekill, including the cantankerous Captain John Avery.

When Avery arrived in the Whorekill, the former sea captain established a homestead of several hundred acres several miles out of town on the north shore of Rehoboth Bay. The retired mariner dubbed his home on the banks of Rehoboth Bay "Avery's Rest," but if Avery and his neighbors believed that the old sea captain would lead a life of quiet leisure, they were wrong. Soon after Avery arrived in the Whorekill, he was appointed as a justice of the peace. The retired mariner, however, spent more time breaking the peace than preserving it.

In 1676, not long after Avery settled on the coast, Edward Southerin, another Whorekill magistrate (justice of the peace), complained to the colonial authorities that Avery called him a "beggarly rogue." In turn, Southerin called Avery a "pitiful fellow" and demanded that he be removed as magistrate. Despite Southerin's plea, Avery continued to serve as a justice of the peace. There were complaints that Avery had performed several marriages without following the proper procedures, that he had released a confessed thief without good cause and that his unruly conduct was unbecoming a justice of the peace. Whenever the other magistrates disagreed with Avery, the former sailor flew into a rage and called "the rest of the court fools, knaves, and rogues." Avery so intimidated the other magistrates that they were afraid to do anything about his belligerent behavior.

In 1680, the court magistrates made a series of requests of the Duke of York's colonial authorities. At the top of their list was an appeal for a tax to raise money for a proper courthouse, prison, stocks and whipping post that would be built in the Whorekill. The court magistrates also requested that the "marsh at the northwest end of the town and the cape [be] common to the use of inhabitants" and that the boundaries of the Whorekill be clarified. The final request, which must have been nagging the inhabitants for some time, was for the colonial authorities "to give the Whorekill some other name."

In January 1681, the colonial government responded by authorizing a new two-story building in the Whorekill to serve as a courthouse. The Second Street building was to be constructed of logs that were at least eight inches thick and topped by "a good strong roof, tight and well-covered." Next to the building stood "a good pair of stocks of nine foot long, and a whipping post at the end of them."

The site selected for the new courthouse was on Second Street next to the house of Philip Russell. Although the authorities issued a detailed description about how the new courthouse was to be built, actual construction on the building did not begin until sometime later. In 1687, the court appealed to the public to supply building materials for the courthouse and prison: "That whoever subscribes any logs to be gotten for the use of the prison and courthouse shall bring the said logs to the place in the town where it is to be built in forty days after the date hereof or else forfeit double the value of said logs." Several of the residents of Lewes pledged to provide the logs needed for the courthouse. Presumably, a proper courthouse was then built with "a good strong roof, tight and well covered."

The court lost no time in hearing cases that the growing number of colonists generated. Many of the cases were complaints about adultery, bigamy, blasphemy, unpaid debts, property lines, swearing, thievery and watered-down beer. In 1683, John Johnson Sr. was suspected of beating his wife, Susan, to death. Because the male court officials did not want to molest Susan's corpse, an unprecedented all-female jury was chosen to examine the body. The twelve women could not discover a single sign of murder, and John Johnson was set free.

While the court was administering justice on the Whorekill, William Penn was petitioning King Charles II for a grant of land in America. William's late father, Admiral Sir William Penn, had been a member of Parliament and a confidant of the king. The king owed the heirs of Sir William the princely sum of £16,000, and William asked for the land north of Maryland and west of the Delaware River to settle that debt. In early 1882, the king agreed to the grant. With Pennsylvania in hand, the Quaker leader then asked the Duke of York for his Delaware lands. In August, the duke agreed, and Penn promptly boarded a ship to inspect his newly acquired holdings.

Arriving at New Castle in October 1682, Penn divided Pennsylvania into three counties and organized three Delaware counties, which he named New Castle, Kent and Sussex. The town of Whorekill was renamed "Lewes" for a town in the English county of Sussex. The peripatetic Penn made trips to New Jersey, Maryland and, in April 1683, Lewes.

While in Lewes, Penn took depositions from several people who had been present when the town was burned by William Howell in 1673. He hoped to use these statements to bolster his case that the Cape Henlopen area was cultivated by Europeans before Lord Baltimore received his grant. Penn also attended a session of the court during which the surviving Dutch settlers swore allegiance to him:

> *This day John Kiphaven, Alexander Moulston, Halmanus Wiltbank, Cornelis Verhoofe, Corneilis Johnson, Francis Henry, Cornelis Plackhoy, Anthony Hamson…having publicly in open court solemnly promised and declared in the presence of God allegiance to the King of England his heirs and successors and fidelity to William Penn, Proprietor and Governor of the province of Pennsylvania.*

After they swore allegiance, Penn "declared all of them to be naturalized as free men of this government as any Englishmen." With that declaration, the colonists acknowledged that the wars between the Dutch and English were over. The border dispute with Maryland lingered, but the argument was in the hands of the lawyers. For now, Lewes was under

The creek front in the early twentieth century. *Courtesy of the Delaware Public Archives.*

the wing of William Penn and the English. The settlement near Cape Henlopen was quickly transformed from a string of farms bordering the Whorekill to the town of Lewes with tight groups of homes lining Front and Second Streets.

## COMMITTING GREAT SPOIL

After the old salt John Avery passed away and Helmanus Wiltbank followed him to the grave, a fresh wave of colonists arrived. Lewes was passed to a new generation of residents. One hundred miles to the north of Cape Henlopen, Philadelphia was fast emerging as a major shipping point, and residents of Lewes found work guiding the ever-increasing number of ships past the sandbars that littered Delaware Bay. Many of these pilots lived near the inlet on the road that paralleled Lewes Creek, and their settlement became known as "Pilottown." With the increased traffic on the bay, the two sailing ships that arrived in 1698 did not attract much notice. They appeared to be another pair of colonial sailing ships, and the residents of Lewes did not suspect anything unusual.

After dropping anchor, several dozen cutthroats rowed ashore and took eleven leaders of the town hostage. The brigands then proceeded to break into houses and systematically strip the town of blankets, clothing, money and anything of value that they could find. After a day plundering Lewes, the pirates retreated to their ships, where they feasted on several hogs and sheep that were taken from the town. With the pirates holding the eleven hostages, the townspeople of Lewes were powerless to act, and they were afraid that the pirates would return to the town for more livestock or "to burn ye houses."

After the people from the town were forced to load stolen goods onto the pirates' ships, the pirates released their hostages, set sail and disappeared into the wide expanse of the Atlantic Ocean. Relieved that the ordeal was over, a delegation of Lewes residents wrote to the colonial authorities, "They are beggarly rogues and will pillage for a trifle…This place is very open to danger and very naked for defense."

A year after pirates ransacked Lewes, a sloop slid quietly into Delaware Bay and dropped anchor in the lee of Cape Henlopen. Satisfied that their arrival had not attracted undue note, the crew of the sloop waited for the arrival of the ship *Saint Antonio* and its captain, the notorious William Kidd.

Unlike the cutthroats who had pillaged Lewes, Captain William Kidd considered himself a gentleman, and he had no intention of molesting the residents of the Delaware town. The buccaneer captain was more interested in protecting the vast treasure that he had accumulated on his voyage to the Indian Ocean and in meeting the small sloop that lay at anchor near Cape Henlopen.

Kidd was born in the middle of the seventeenth century, and he had gone to sea as a young man. His homeport was New York City, and after Kidd had married the widow of a prominent merchant, the ambitious mariner gained prominence by helping to suppress the pirates who sailed along the New England Coast. In 1695, Richard Bellomont, governor of New York, commissioned Kidd to outfit an armed vessel as a privateer to quell the pirates who raided English ships in the Indian Ocean. In colonial America, a privateer was a privately owned vessel that had a legal commission to attack enemy ships. Unfortunately for William Kidd, the line between privateer and pirate was easily crossed.

After Kidd sailed to the Indian Ocean, he captured several ships, but apparently, his crewmen were not satisfied by the loot that they had taken. Kidd stopped at Madagascar, where a substantial portion of Kidd's crew deserted. Believing that further efforts in the Indian Ocean would be useless, Kidd decided to return to New York. On his way home, he stopped at Lewes and rendezvoused with a small sloop that was anchored near Cape Henlopen. After the *Saint Antonio* dropped anchor off Lewes, the pirate captain welcomed several sailors from the sloop aboard his ship, and the transfer of some of the loot from the *Saint Antonio* began. As the pirates worked, one of the cutthroats, James Kelly, had his eye on the high dunes of Cape Henlopen.

Kelly was an everyday pirate who spent his days afloat scheming and robbing until he ran afoul of the authorities. Like most rogues of the sea, Kelly did much to hide his past and his identity. He sometimes sailed under his true name, but other times, he called himself "James Gilliam" and "Sampson Marshall." After he was captured and sentenced to death for piracy, Kelly wrote an account of his nefarious activities with the cumbersome, but romantic title *A Full and True Discovery of All the Robberies, Pyracies, and other Notorious Actions of that Famous English Pyrate, Capt. James Kelly.*

Kelly joined Kidd's crew in Madagascar, and he was with the pirate captain when he dropped anchor near Lewes. Some time later, Edward Davis, one of Kidd's crewmen, swore that "upon their arrival at the Whorekill, in Delaware Bay, there was a chest belonging to one James Gilliam put ashore there."

While in Lewes, a resident of the town wrote to the British colonial authorities, "Capt. Kidd is come into this bay; he hath been here about 10 days, he sends his boat ashore to the Hore Kills in this government, where he is supplied with what he wants; and the people frequently go on board her." George Thompson, Peter Lewis and William Orr were among the Lewes residents who boarded the pirate ship, where they were dazzled by the calico, muslin, sugar and other goods. In addition, they reported that there were tons of gold aboard the ship. Thompson, Lewes and Orr were suspected of buying and bringing some of Kidd's loot ashore.

After Kidd sailed from Lewes, he continued on to Boston, where he was charged with piracy, arrested and carted off to England for trial. When he had difficulty producing documentation that he had acted as a legal privateer, Kidd was found guilty of piracy and sent to the gallows After Kidd's execution, William Penn was far more lenient toward the three men from Lewes who had collaborated with the pirate. Penn had Thompson, Lewis and Orr arrested, but they maintained that they had boarded Kidd's vessel as honest merchants. The Quaker leader ordered, "Such men must not be endured to live near ye sea-coast nor trade, least they become receptacles, and brokers for younger pirates."

## A Poet, a Priest and a Judge

While Lewes was playing host to Captain Kidd and boatloads of cutthroats, other ships were sailing past Cape Henlopen packed with settlers bound for Philadelphia. The City of Brotherly Love was only two decades old, but it already contained seven thousand inhabitants and was rapidly becoming colonial America's largest city. In 1702, Henry Brooke, the scion of a well-to-do British family, armed with a letter of introduction and the endorsement of a high colonial official, arrived in Philadelphia. He expected to land a cushy job that would enable him to sample the Pennsylvania city's growing number of taverns.

Brooke had attended Oxford, where, between bouts of heavy drinking and carousing, he learned to read ancient writers in the original Greek and Latin. Henry's extracurricular behavior caused the family to banish him to America, where he was appointed port collector at Lewes. When Brooke arrived in Lewes, he found several dozen small houses that lined two streets that paralleled the creek. The Sussex County courthouse was the most important building in town, but the hottest spot in town was next to the courthouse, where Philip Russell's tavern stood at the corner of Second and Mulberry Streets. Russell had been hauled into court for "suffering persons to play at cards" in his establishment. The Lewes tavern owner pleaded that it was "my first offense, and happened much against my will, so strong were the card players." It was just the place for Henry Brooke.

If the activities at Russell's tavern were not enough to amuse the exiled aristocrat, Brooke could hitch a ride aboard a ship bound for Philadelphia, where the nightlife would be more to his taste. In his poem "To My Bottle Friends," the bon vivant Brooke celebrated the joys of the tavern: "The wine and company are good, another flask, another hour; such juice is Wit's peculiar food, and Wit's sociable power." In 1703, however, Brooke drank another flask and stayed another hour too late, and he was arrested for "creating a great disturbance and riot in the streets after the hour of midnight." Brooke paid a small fine for disturbing the peace of the City of Brotherly Love, and properly chastised, he returned home to Lewes.

Not all of Brooke's trips to Philadelphia were tavern-crawling expeditions. In 1709, when a French privateer appeared off Cape Henlopen, the residents of Lewes feared that they would suffer a repeat of the 1698 pirate plundering of the town. Before the privateer attacked Lewes, Brooke set sail for Philadelphia. At the same time, another Lewes resident, Richard Westly, had spotted the arrival of the French privateer. Westly also took a small boat and began to sail up the bay. As he made his way to Philadelphia, Westly gave "notice to all ye outward bound vessels, that he could possibly speak with, that they might avoid the danger."

When Brooke reached Philadelphia, he pleaded with the colonial authorities for help in protecting Lewes. When they failed to act promptly,

Brooke hired two ships and returned to the town. He intended to drive off the privateers, but they had already left by the time that his two ships reached Cape Henlopen.

Unlike Brooke, Westly remained in Philadelphia, where he delivered a bill to the colonial government for his expenses. Westly believed that he should be "satisfied for his own and his companions' trouble."

Shortly after this incident, a frigate of the British Royal Navy was assigned to patrol the mouth of Delaware Bay, and the reports of pirates in the area began to decline. Lewes became a more peaceful town, and Henry Brooke began to mellow. His merrymaking trips to Philadelphia declined, and the college dropout began to spend more time in his library. With his playboy days behind him, Brooke developed a reputation as a respected man of knowledge. In 1717, He became Speaker of the House of Representatives in the Lower Counties, and in 1721, he was appointed to the Governor's Council. Five years later, Brooke was appointed as a judge in the colonial Supreme Court.

The same year that Brooke was appointed to the Governor's Council, he met Reverend William Becket, who shared his interest in literature. In 1721, Becket was dispatched as an Anglican missionary to Sussex County, and the English cleric assumed the rectorship of St. Peter's Episcopal Parish, which owned four acres of land between Market and Mulberry Streets with fronting on Second Street. The church land stood adjacent to the courthouse and the site of Philip Russell's tavern. One of Becket's duties as rector was to oversee the completion of a church building that stood near the entrance to the churchyard on Second Street. In addition to the St. Peter's, a Presbyterian congregation worshiped at a church on King's Highway. Around the time that Becket began to hold services in St. Peter's, Philip Russell sold his tavern, and it passed into the hands of a young merchant named Ryves Holt. For the next several decades, much of the activity in Lewes would be focused on the block of Second Street between Market and Mulberry, where the church, courthouse and Ryves Holt's house stood.

Born in 1696, Ryves Holt had lived in Philadelphia, where he was engaged in the West Indies trade, before he moved to Lewes to accept an appointment as the naval officer of the port. In this position, Holt checked on all vessels entering or leaving Delaware Bay. Like Henry Brooke, Holt held a variety of government positions, among them, chief justice of the colonial Delaware Supreme Court. Holt also became a friend of William Becket and, presumably, Henry Brooke as well.

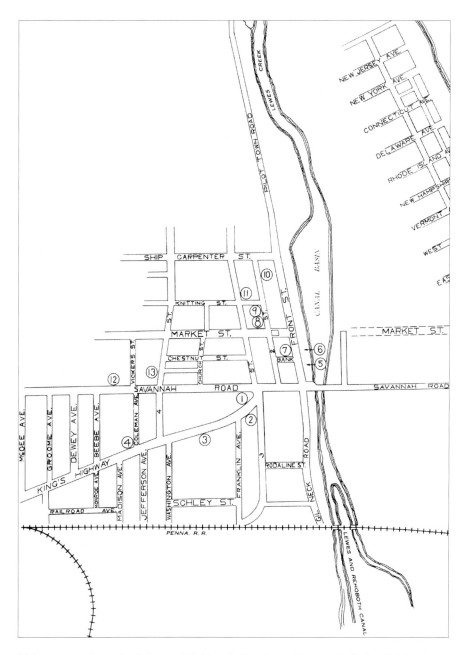

This map was drawn for *Delaware: A Guide to the First State* written by the Federal Writers' Project, a part of the New Deal's Works Projects Administration, and published in 1938. Significant sites indicated are (1) Zwaanendael Museum, (3) Lewes Presbyterian Church, (5) Memorial Park, (8) St. Peter's Episcopal Church and (9) Ryves Holt House. *Courtesy of the Delaware Public Archives.*

Holt, Brooke and Becket were the literati of Lewes, and Becket felt the fifty-eight families of the town needed access to a weekly newspaper. Consequently, the rector of St. Peter's led a petition to have Ben Franklin's *Pennsylvania Gazette* delivered to Lewes regularly. Becket shared Brooke's interest in poetry, and the two became good friends. When Brooke died in 1735, he bequeathed Becket his library of books, which included volumes in English, French, Greek and Latin. In turn, Becket wrote a poetic tribute to his friend that was published in a Philadelphia newspaper, the *Weekly Mercury*: "Good humor, manly wit, a gen'rous mind, a judgment strong, a fancy unconfined, a friend to virtue and a foe to vice, in all thy conduct regularly nice. Happy the future age, that once shall see in all respects a parallel to thee!"

Four years after Henry Brooke passed away, the charismatic priest and preacher George Whitefield arrived in Lewes, and Reverend Becket was not pleased. Whitefield's thundering voice and fiery sermons had already earned the twenty-four-year-old preacher a booming reputation. Arriving by pilot boat, Whitefield preached at St. Peter's, where he attracted a larger-than-expected congregation for a town the size of Lewes. Whitefield's loud and clear voice made it possible for an enormous number of people to hear him. On Whitefield's second visit to Lewes, St. Peter's could not accommodate the huge throng that gathered to hear him, and Whitefield preached to the crowd outside from a balcony. Reverend Becket was appalled. The rector of St. Peter's condemned Whitefield for breaking ecclesiastical protocol by leaving the church building. Whitefield and other Great Awakening preachers confronted their listeners with shocking images of the horrors that awaited sinners in the afterlife. Becket sarcastically commented that Whitefield had thrown so much fire and brimstone about that he was afraid that he would ignite the wooden frame church. "I conclude," Becket added, "that enthusiasm is a sort of a wild fire that leads men into ponds and ditches and for all that the muddy fellows think they are in a good road."

The fire of enthusiasm that Whitefield ignited in Lewes had cooled considerably by the time that Reverend Becket guided St. Peter's through two decades of growth, until he passed away in 1743. In his will, Becket requested that he be buried between his two wives in St. Peter's churchyard, dividing his holdings—including his two slaves, Jenny and Oxford—among his surviving relatives, and to his friend Ryves Holt, he bequeathed "a gold ring on my ring finger."

Holt continued to live in the house on the corner of Second and Mulberry Streets, and in 1760, when he was sixty-four years old, he was one of the

Second Street in the early twentieth century. *Courtesy of the Delaware Public Archives.*

commissioners appointed to oversee the surveying team that marked the border between Delaware and Maryland. With that border firmly established, Holt and the people of Lewes could rest assured that their town was not on Lord Baltimore's land. Three years later, Ryves Holt died, leaving a wife, Catherine, and a daughter, Penelope, who continued to live in the house at Second and Mulberry Streets.

## I GOT CLEAR OF THE MOB

"I have the pleasure to inform you," Captain Andrew Snape Hamond, commander of the HMS *Roebuck*, wrote in June 1776, "that the inhabitants of the two lower counties on the Delaware, tired of the tyranny and oppression of the times have taken up arms to the number of three thousand and declared themselves in favor of the [the British] government." The British captain was confident that he could raise six or seven thousand Tories and march on Philadelphia.

When Captain Andrew Snape Hamond arrived at Delaware Bay, he was a twenty-year veteran of the British Royal Navy. In 1776, Hamond was a competent mariner as he guided the frigate *Roebuck* and a squadron of smaller vessels around Cape Henlopen. The British commander intended to squelch the Patriot cause in Delaware by controlling the waters of the bay where Henry Fisher scrambled to organize the defense of Sussex County.

Dr. Henry Fisher, a native of Ireland, arrived in Lewes in 1725, and joined Henry Brooke, Reverend William Becket and Ryves Holt as one of the literati of southern Delaware. Dr. Fisher was one of the first formally educated physicians to live in Sussex County, and he had built an English-style home that reflected his high standing in the community. Ten years after Dr. Fisher arrived in Delaware, Henry was born.

Henry was only twelve years old when his father died in 1748, and it was expected that he would follow in his father's footsteps and become a physician. But the allure of the sea was too strong for him to resist. As a young man, Fisher mastered the shoals and shallows of the Delaware, and he developed into one of the bay's leading pilots. By the 1760s, Philadelphia had developed into the largest city in colonial America, and ships headed for the Pennsylvania city had to navigate around the dangerous shoals that surrounded Cape Henlopen. At the urging of Philadelphia merchants, a lighthouse was constructed at Cape Henlopen, and Fisher selected the site for the beacon on a high dune that loomed over forty feet above the beach. The tower was built of granite, cut from quarries in northern Delaware and transported down the bay to Lewes, where it was transferred to barges that could navigate the shallow waters of the creek. The barges transported the granite to a stone wharf within two miles of the construction area. Teams of oxen hauled the stone up the high dunes to the lighthouse site, and when the beacon was finished in 1765, the Cape Henlopen Lighthouse was the tallest structure south of Philadelphia. The base of the lighthouse was twenty-six feet in diameter, and the lower walls were six feet thick. The sturdy eight-sided tower was over sixty-nine feet tall. Inside the tower, a winding wooden staircase threaded its way past seven landings to the keeper's room that was just below the room that contained the whale-oil lantern. The keeper used a ladder to climb up to the eighth level, where he tended to the lantern and its reflectors.

In 1776, the Cape Henlopen Lighthouse provided mariners an unmistakable landmark to navigate their vessels. As Captain Hamond aboard the *Roebuck* led his small flotilla of British warships into Delaware Bay, he encountered Henry Fisher and a meager collection of poorly trained Patriot forces. Many able-bodied Patriots in Sussex County had already marched off to join General George Washington's Continental army, so there were relatively few Patriots left in Lewes. In addition, southern Delaware's Tories threatened to unite with Hamond's naval force to overthrow the local Patriot authorities. Fisher's

Standing atop a high dune, the Cape Henlopen lighthouse guided mariners for over a century and a half. *Courtesy of the Delaware Public Archives.*

knowledge of coastal waters, however, gave the Patriot pilot an advantage that Hamond and the strongest navy in the world did not possess.

As soon as Hamond's squadron entered the bay, some of Fisher's men lit lanterns at the Cape Henlopen Lighthouse and fired a gun to indicate that British warships were approaching. Fisher also established a system of relay riders who carried dispatches from Lewes to the Continental Congress in Philadelphia. When Hamond led a squadron of warships into Delaware Bay, Fisher immediately sent an express rider to Philadelphia. His dispatch on the arrival of the *Roebuck* alerted the American authorities in Pennsylvania that the British might be headed up the bay. Without a pilot to guide him, however, Hamond's ship ran aground several times. In addition, small American gunboats harassed the British ships at every opportunity, and the frustrated Hamond retreated down the bay to Cape Henlopen.

Fisher's reports on the movements of Hamond's ships and accounts of the growing strength of the Tories in southern Delaware prompted the Congress to order a detachment of Patriot troops to the coastal region, and several small gunboats were sent to the waters off Lewes. In addition, Caesar Rodney left the deliberations over the Declaration of Independence to hurry south. Rodney and the troops were able to prevent the Tory attempt to gain control of Sussex County. Rodney did not travel as far south as Lewes, but his hasty return to the congress to vote for independence has become a cherished part of Delaware lore. Once the Continental Congress declared independence on July 4, 1776, a rider was dispatched to Lewes. A few days later, William Adair, of Lewes, wrote in his journal: "An express from Congress—Independence proclaimed at ye Head of ye Delaware Battalion—July 10 with 3 cheers." Ten days later, the residents of Sussex County were still celebrating the break with England. Adair noted: "July 20. Independence declared at Lewes, 3 Cannon discharged and 3 Toasts."

In defiance of the growing number of Tories loitering inland, the Lewes Patriots set up a Liberty Pole topped by the new flag of the United States near Fisher's house. The flag was flying proudly on election day in October 1776 and was nearly fatal for Henry Fisher. In the eighteenth century, voters were required to come to Lewes to cast their votes at the courthouse, and the influx of people made some elections rollicking affairs. On election day, merchants set up booths to sell food and drinks to the throng of voters, and the free-flowing alcohol lubricated an already raucous crowd. In 1776, the usually abrasive election day behavior was further aroused by the passions of the American Revolution, and an estimated 650 Loyalists came to Lewes looking for a fight. Although he was well known as a leading patriot, Fisher was not intimidated by the hordes of Tories parading through the streets of Lewes. He sat by his front door where he could see the Liberty Pole and watch the boisterous Loyalists.

Around noon, one of the Tory bullies marched up to Fisher and demanded an axe so that he could cut down the Liberty Pole. Fisher refused. The Loyalist grabbed Fisher and began to drag him into the street. As the two men tussled, a friend of Fisher's intervened, and Fisher later wrote, "By struggling and the assistance of some friend, I got clear of the mob and safe into my house, where I was obliged to keep close the remaining part of the day; the mob threatening to roast me alive if they could get me into the street."

Unable to get to Fisher, the mob went away, but a short time later, they returned and cut down the Liberty Pole. According to Fisher:

> *They then took the top of the pole, on which part of the Independent flag had been us'd to be hoisted, and carried in derision about the town, followed by the crowd throwing up their hats and huzzaing for the king, when tired with that kind of mockery, set it up a public sale, struck it off it is said for thirteen pence, meaning I supposed hangman's wages.*

As the Tories made their way to the courthouse to vote, one of the gang, armed with a large hickory club, stationed himself at the courthouse door and declared that only those who supported the king would be allowed to

*Lewes Harbor, 1784.* The figure seated in the center of the small boat is the Patriot and pilot Henry Fisher. *Courtesy of PNC Collection by the late artist Robert Goodier.*

enter and to vote. Fisher observed: "Thus forcibly electing a number of their junta to represent them in the General Assembly." When the voting was concluded for the day, the Tories left Lewes, and it was safe for Fisher to come out of his barricaded house.

Six months after Fisher's harrowing experience on election day, the morning fog was lifting as the HMS *Roebuck* sailed quietly off Cape Henlopen. On the other side of the cape, Captain James Anderson guided the *Morris* through the dissipating fog toward the mouth of the bay. The *Morris* was carrying a cargo of military goods that included thirty-five tons of gunpowder destined for General George Washington's Continental army. When Hamond spotted the American ship, he ordered the *Roebuck* and a smaller British warship to intercept the *Morris*. Aboard the *Morris*, Captain Anderson saw the approaching British warships, and he steered for the Cape Henlopen Lighthouse, apparently seeking the shallow water where the larger British ships could not follow. Hamond, however, ordered the *Roebuck* to open fire, and for several hours, the English warships showered Anderson's vessel with cannon balls.

After several hours of desperate combat, the British bombardment began to have an effect, and Anderson saw that he could not hold out much longer. He beached the *Morris* on the sand of Cape Henlopen and then ordered a powder train to be laid to the cargo of gunpowder. As much of the crew scrambled over the bow to shore, Anderson lit a fuse to the powder train. Moments later, the *Morris* exploded in a deafening roar.

In his autobiography, Captain Hamond recalled, "When she blew up with a most terrible explosion, [the ship formed] a column of liquid fire to a great height, and then spread into a head of black smoke, showering down burn pieces of wood &c which covered a space round about for near ½ a mile on the water."

On shore, Henry Fisher watched as the *Morris* vainly attempted to elude the British. He said of Anderson, "finding he could defend her no longer, he laid a train & blew the ship up, and I am sorry to tell you that so brave a Man has fell in the attempt." Fisher also reported: "The cargo is in part blown shore, viz. Guns, Clothes, Gun Locks…We have [a] number of men saving the Cargo." It appears that no effort was made to salvage the *Morris* and the remains of Captain James Anderson, which were allowed to settle into the sands of Cape Henlopen.

Early in the war, Captain David Hall, a resident of Lewes, commanded a small force that defended the cape and the lighthouse. Hall's men built a series of gun emplacements; but before the earthworks were finished, most of the troops were ordered to join the Continental army in New York. A company of less than one hundred men, along with several small American gunboats that harassed the British ships at every opportunity, remained in the Cape Henlopen area to keep watch on the *Roebuck* and other British ships.

Although they were short-handed, the small group of soldiers worked to complete the earthworks and guard the Cape Henlopen Lighthouse. The troops always had their muskets, cartridge boxes and other equipment close at hand while they were working to construct the earthworks. The soldiers were ordered to be alert for the sound of two cannons fired in quick succession. When they heard that signal, the troops would throw down their picks, shovels and other tools, snatch up their muskets and military equipment and hurry to Lewes, where they would expect to meet a British attack.

Although the British did not make a concerted effort to attack Lewes, Hamond occasionally ordered men ashore to obtain supplies. Allegedly, British sailors asked the keeper of the Cape Henlopen lighthouse for cattle that were grazing nearby, and the keeper defiantly replied, "I'll give you no cows, but if you don't get out, I'll give you some bullets!" Though the

St. Peter's Epicopal Church on Second Street. The current building was constructed in the mid-nineteenth century and is surrounded by numerous historic tombstones. *Photo by Michael Morgan.*

sailors meekly left, they later returned with reinforcements and burned the lighthouse's interior and destroyed the beacon's lamps. (The incident is not mentioned the *Roebuck*'s ship logs, which casts doubt on this story. It may be that some accident with the lamp fuel caused the fire that burned the wooden staircase inside the lighthouse.) The tower remained darkened for the remainder of the war.

## WHEN YOU GO

Although there are some areas along Pilottown Road where you can get a glimpse of the beach and the bay, the development of Lewes and the area across the canal has blocked the view of the sea. On many of the town's streets, there is no longer a feeling that Lewes is perched on the edge of the bay. On Second Street, St. Peter's Church (the present building was erected in the 1850s) is surrounded by the graves of many of its historic parishioners and others. On King's Highway, the Presbyterian congregation worships in a building that was dedicated in 1832, and it, too, is encircled by the graves of many historic parishioners.

The site of the Sussex County courthouse. The building in the right background is the Ryves Holt House. *Photo by Michael Morgan.*

The Ryves Holt House, now an information center for the Lewes Historical Society. To the left is a picket fence in front of the site of the Sussex County courthouse. *Photo by Michael Morgan.*

Known as Fisher's Paradise, the home of Lewes pilot and Patriot Henry Fisher sits on Pilottown Road. Samuel Boyer Davis, who commanded the defense of Lewes during the War of 1812, also lived here. *Photo by Michael Morgan.*

The courthouse where John Avery railed against other Lewes residents was torn down long ago, and the land on Second Street has been reincorporated into St. Peter's churchyard. On the corner of Second and Mulberry Streets, Ryves Holt House, however, still stands as it did when pirates roamed the streets, Lewes residents traded with Captain Kidd and Jacob Jones developed a yearning for the sea. The building now serves as an information center and gift shop for the Lewes Historical Society.

Christopher Ward, the eminent Delaware historian, wrote of Henry Fisher, "No other man in Delaware and few in the American colonies worked harder, more constantly and more effectively for the cause of the American Independence, with so little of glory and renown as a posthumous reward." Over the years, there have been several attempts to raise a fitting monument to Fisher, but to no avail. Fisher's house, however, remains on Pilottown Road and is a private residence.

# Chapter 3

# ON THE STREETS OF LEWES

## WITH COLORS FLYING

The end of the American Revolution did not end the animosity between the residents of Lewes and those who lived in the interior of Sussex County. Ten years after the Tories invaded Lewes on election day and threatened to roast Henry Fisher alive, another mob of voters armed with pistols, swords and clubs came to town, planning to vote and looking for a fight.

As the armed men crowded into Lewes on October 1, 1787, Sussex County sheriff Peter Wright stood in front of the courthouse on Second Street and read the 1779 law granting him the authority to postpone the voting. When he ended his announcement, Wright declared that the polls would not open that day, and he scampered out of town to Dover to confer with Delaware president (governor) Thomas Collins.

Later that day, Wright arrived in Dover and met with Collins, who issued a proclamation decrying the unruly behavior in Lewes and requiring all government officials to assist in the suppression of riotous activity so as to ensure a free and fair election. Sheriff Wright returned to Lewes that night and posted Collins's proclamation in time to disperse a group of newly arrived armed men.

The rescheduled election was to be held on October 8, with President Collins in attendance to observe the proceedings. Before the voting began, however, James Trusham led a party of 150 horsemen down Second Street to the courthouse. Sheriff Wright immediately consulted President Collins, promptly closed the polls and headed to a tavern for a drink. When scuffles began outside the tavern, Wright declared himself sick and went to bed.

The election was again rescheduled for the following week under a unique arrangement during which only fifty voters from the two contending factions would be allowed to vote. When the hundred votes had been cast, Undersheriff Thomas Laws, who was supervising the election in place of the bedridden Sheriff Wright, declared the voting closed. Laws and an election inspector from Cedar Creek Hundred went to the second floor of Hercules Kollock's house, where they were surprised by a group of men who beat them with clubs. Laws was able to escape by running down the stairs, and the election inspector fled by jumping out a window. Meanwhile, an eyewitness reported that the irrepressible James Trusham arrived in Lewes and struck Thomas Evans so violently that Evans crumpled into a heap. The unconscious Evans recovered, but alerted by his misfortune, many of the residents of Lewes fled to avoid the armed thugs. When the militia arrived to keep order, some complained that they entered Lewes "with colors flying, and themselves furnished with pistols, clubs, cutlasses &c to the great terror of the peaceable inhabitants of said town, and did then and there beat and wound several people."

The state legislature voided the election and ordered a new one to be held elsewhere. For the first time, voting was to be held outside Lewes at Vaughan's Furnace in Nanticoke Hundred in central Sussex County. The election at Vaughn's Furnace was little different from that held in Lewes. Hundreds of armed men milled about the town and threatened to shoot those who disagreed with them. Some of these ruffians were led by James Trusham, who had laid Thomas Evans low in the streets of Lewes. On election day at Vaughn's Furnace, Trusham again appeared and continued to harass voters. The night after the voting had been completed, Sheriff Peter Wright, sufficiently recovered from his illness, barricaded the polling place because he believed that a mob of armed men was lurking in the area.

The mob never appeared, and a much-relieved Sheriff Wright was able to report the results without incident. The election at Vaughan's Furnace was considered a success, and it marked the beginning of the end for Lewes as the dominant force in southern Delaware politics. The residents of the interior revived a decades-old desire to move the county seat from Lewes to an inland location. In 1769, residents of western Sussex County suggested moving the county seat to Milton, which was then known as Cross Roads. The citizens of Lewes vigorously defend their town, and

John Rodney wrote a letter to his cousin, Caesar, that emphasized the town's geographic advantages:

> *Lewes town is the most suitable place I apprehend in this county for the publick buildings; we have opportunities almost every week for nine months of the year to send for necessaries to Philadelphia. There are many able farmers near Lewes who can supply the town with other necessaries; besides the advantage of the fisheries—neither of which is the case at the Cross Roads—Lewes is pleasantly situated and esteemed a very healthy place, and the land is good in [and] about the town for five miles round.*

The debate over the suitability of Lewes to host government functions heightened toward the end of the American Revolution, when the Delaware General Assembly decided to meet in Lewes. Some of the lawmakers were apprehensive about the quality of the accommodations that they would find in Lewes, but James Booth was pleased with the town. He wrote to Caesar Rodney:

> *The air of Lewes at present seems very clear, and free from those damp vapors that I apprehended Sea-Air was generally impregnated with…Accommodations and table are very good, nay they very much surpass my expectations and equal my wishes. Major Fisher has also provided a quantity of good claret and fruit, which with Rehoboth Oysters &c. tend to make the place more agreeable.*

The contentious elections, the location of Lewes in a far corner of the county and the growing political power of the noncoastal residents convinced the state legislature to authorize the relocation of the county seat from Lewes to a more central site. In 1791, a group of commissioners acquired land and laid out the new town, which was dubbed "Georgetown," to serve as the new county seat. When the courthouse closed in Lewes, it ended an era that had begun in the seventeenth century, when Lewes had served as the center of political and legal activity for southern Delaware. Lewes would survive, but without the courthouse where elections were held and cases were adjudicated, the town would never be the same.

# A Knife Fight, Gunshots and a Hot Temper

With the loss of the county seat, fewer southern Delaware residents visited Lewes, but the town managed to garner a healthy share of visitors. In 1793, Stephen Girard, the prominent Philadelphia merchant, had fallen on hard times before he arrived in town. Hounded by creditors, the Philadelphia entrepreneur believed that he had spotted an opportunity to rebuild his fortune. In Haiti, a slave revolt left many businessmen and plantation owners desperate for a way to flee the island with their valuables. Girard left Philadelphia on a ship bound for the troubled island and stopped at Lewes. When Girard's Philadelphia creditors learned that he had left the city, they were enraged. They obtained a writ for his arrest, and they dispatched a rider with it to Lewes, where the writ was delivered to Sheriff Thomas Fisher, who set out to arrest Girard.

When Fisher confronted Girard, the merchant flew into a rage, drew a knife and lunged at Fisher. The sheriff neatly parried Girard's knife with one hand, and with his other hand, Fisher knocked Girard to the floor. After a brief struggle, the sheriff disarmed the merchant and hustled him through the streets of Lewes to the town jail.

Once behind bars, Girard regained his composure, and he was allowed to post bail. The merchant sailed to the West Indies, where was able to earn enough money transporting anxious plantation owners and others to America that he was able to satisfy his creditors and rebuild his fortune. When he died in 1831, he left much of his money to charity, but many in Lewes continued to talk about the time that he had a knife fight with Sheriff Fisher.

While Stephen Girard was attempting to rebuild his finances at knifepoint, Dr. Theodore Wilson was quietly visiting his patients, or so it seemed. Theodore Wilson was the second son of the ardent patriot and pillar of the Lewes community Dr. Matthew Wilson, a prominent physician and clergyman who was also the pastor of the Presbyterian church in Lewes on King's Highway. When the American Revolution began, Matthew's strong feelings about the colonial cause prompted him to write the word "Patriot" on the crown of his hat. Theodore was born in 1772. He had a difficult time measuring up to his father's example. In addition, Theodore had to compete with his older brother and his father's favorite son, James Patriot Wilson.

Although not as brilliant as his father, Theodore was apparently a competent doctor who built a respectable practice in Lewes and the surrounding area. In 1792, Wilson's devotion to his duty as a physician compelled him to make the ten- to fifteen-mile trek over the notoriously bad roads of Sussex

County to treat James Wiley, an easygoing Irish immigrant. Night had fallen when Wilson reached the Wiley home, where the good doctor found James confined to bed with a fever, which Wilson had little difficulty treating. The young doctor also had little problem getting acquainted with Wiley's wife, Nancy. After James Wiley recovered, Theodore and Nancy continued to see each other frequently. James, who was a good-natured but unperceptive fellow, failed to notice that his wife was having an affair with Theodore.

Two years after Nancy began seeing the doctor regularly, Wiley made an ill-advised move to Lewes, where he opened a tavern. Relocating to Lewes not only enabled Nancy to see Dr. Wilson more frequently but also allowed her to strike up more than a passing acquaintance with a number of other men in town.

The affair between the doctor and the tavern keeper's wife simmered for five years. In 1799, Nancy, who may have grown weary of gossip about her behavior, left Lewes, her husband and Wilson and headed for Philadelphia. Wiley, who seems to have ignored all the rumors about his wife's infidelity, followed Nancy to Philadelphia and brought her back to Lewes. Wilson also went to Philadelphia, where he questioned Nancy's friends about reports that Wiley was mistreating her.

Once he had Nancy back in Lewes, Wiley apparently locked her in a room to keep her from seeing other men. Wiley's life was steadily disintegrating. His tavern business had collapsed, his marriage was a sham and he had become the butt of salacious talk throughout Lewes. Finally convinced that Wilson had more than a professional interest in his wife, Wiley decided to confront Wilson.

The meeting between the tavern keeper and the doctor did not go well. Wilson told Wiley he had reason to believe that Nancy was being mistreated. Wiley took umbrage at the accusation, and the conversation degenerated to the point that the only thing they could agree on was a duel to settle the matter. Before the *affaire d'honneur* could be held, however, Wilson backed out.

Despite the efforts of some of Wilson's friends to convince him to end the relationship with Mrs. Wiley, they continued the affair. The thoroughly frustrated Wiley was infuriated when he learned that a meeting had been called by the Masonic lodge to discuss the situation. On December 6, 1799, Wilson and several of the leading citizens of Lewes gathered at Elliott's Tavern, which was housed in the building that had once been the county courthouse.

At the meeting, Wilson sat in front of a fireplace with his head down and holding a small cane. Among those in attendance were Colonel David

Hall, who would be elected governor in 1802, and other prominent Lewes citizens. The doctor listened quietly as his affair with Nancy was discussed and debated. Meanwhile, Wiley had learned of the meeting, put a pistol into his pocket and hurried to Elliott's Tavern. When he entered the tavern, Wilson was still seated facing the fireplace and did not notice Wiley's arrival. Some of the men invited Wiley to have a seat in front of the fire, but he refused. Instead, he drew his pistol, walked up behind Wilson and blew the philandering doctor's brains out. The others in the room grabbed Wiley, who made no effort to resist. The tavern keeper was arrested, tried, found guilty of murder and sentenced to be hanged.

While Wiley awaited his fate, a number of petitions were sent to Governor Richard Bassett urging leniency. Wiley's case had been heard by a troika of three judges, and Governor Bassett asked one of the judges, Kensey Johns, for a recommendation. Johns reported that while Wiley had, in fact, killed Wilson, the tavern keeper had been grossly provoked by the doctor. According to Johns, Wilson had driven Wiley to drink, destroyed his marriage and led to the decline of his business. On April 13, 1800, Bassett signed a pardon for Wiley.

Although freed from the hangman's noose, Wiley's life remained in tatters. Nancy again fled to Philadelphia, and this time, he could not get her to return home. The tavern keeper went back to Lewes, where both his mental and physical health continued to degenerate. Wiley's escape from the gallows, however, enraged Dr. Wilson's older brother, James. In a scene that mirrored the doctor's death, James Wilson confronted Wiley, produced a gun and aimed it at Wiley's head. When the doctor's brother pulled the trigger, the flint snapped forward, but the weapon failed to fire. As Wiley was hustled away, Wilson, his honor apparently restored, laconically remarked, "I tried anyway!"

The Wilson-Wiley affair was the talk of southern Delaware for years, and it was likely heard by Parson Mason Weems, who visited Lewes in 1808. Weems is well known as the writer of the popular biography of George Washington that includes the fictional cherry tree story, which Weems used to illustrate the value of telling the truth. Weems was on the lookout for good stories to demonstrate morals and used the Wiley-Wilson affair as the basis for *God's Revenge against Adultery*, which had to go through four editions to satisfy demand.

Lewes had hardly recovered from the Wiley-Wilson affair when the acid-tongued Betsy Patterson arrived in town for a visit. At the start of the nineteenth century, Betsy's father, William Patterson, was one of the richest men in

America. A merchant, real estate broker and shipbuilder, Patterson helped Baltimore become the third-largest city in America, and in return, a large park on the east side of that town was named for him. Patterson hobnobbed with the elite of American society, and his daughter, Elizabeth (who was sometimes referred to as "bewitching Betsy"), often accompanied him.

Betsy Patterson was well acquainted with her father's business transactions, spoke passable French and was astonishingly beautiful and relentlessly ambitious. She also possessed a will of iron and a fiery tongue. She hated Baltimore, and once declared that "I would have married the devil to get out of Baltimore." Then she met Jerome Bonaparte, Napoleon's little brother.

Jerome, nicknamed "Fifi," was handsome, capricious, irresponsible and incredibly stupid. While Napoleon was methodically conquering most of Europe, he installed his many brothers on thrones across the Continent, but Napoleon was leery of Fifi's royal prowess. Jerome was dispatched on an extended tour of America, where the dull and handsome Fifi met the cunning and beautiful Betsy. Quicker than Napoleon could conquer a country, Betsy and Jerome were married. During the ceremony, which was held on Christmas Eve 1803, Jerome wore a stunning suit of purple satin and diamond buckles, and Betsy's dress was a gossamer gown composed of so little fabric that a witness said it could have been stuffed into a pocket and used as a handkerchief.

After an extended honeymoon, the newlyweds set sail for Europe, where Betsy expected to meet the Bonaparte family and cavort with the social elite. The young couple left Philadelphia and sailed happily down Delaware Bay, but a contrary wind forced them to stop at Lewes. If Betsy hated Baltimore, which was one of America's largest cities, Mrs. Bonaparte was appalled by Lewes. The quiet little Delaware town perched behind the high dunes of Cape Henlopen had only a couple hundred inhabitants who lived in modest homes that lined a few muddy streets.

Betsy's introduction to Lewes was not auspicious. After the ship carrying Betsy and Jerome was delayed at Lewes, the young couple demanded to be taken ashore. According to one version of the incident, the small boat carrying Betsy capsized in Lewes Creek, and a Lewes pilot, Shelby Hickman, pulled fiery Betsy to safety. To say the least, her near drowning put Betsy in a foul mood as the newlyweds trekked down Pilottown Road to the Maul house, where the excited residents of Lewes held a dinner in honor of the famous couple. Unfortunately, Betsy found the table setting to be unbecoming a member of Europe's most powerful family. The candlesticks were not up to her standards, and dinner was delayed while servants were dispatched to the

Bonapartes' ship, where silver candlesticks were procured. During the delay, when one of the more pious members of the town apparently remarked that if Betsy had not been pulled from Lewes Creek, she would be in heaven, Betsy snapped, "I would rather be in the court of France than live in the kingdom of heaven."

Having insulted the lifestyle and shocked the sensibilities of the people of Lewes, Betsy and Fifi returned to their ship and set sail to Europe, where Napoleon was furious that his brother had married without his permission. Napoleon ordered the ports of Europe closed to Betsy, and the marriage was annulled. When she finally landed in Europe, Betsy was shunned by the ruling classes. She spent the rest of her life seeking the imperial title that had just barely eluded her. Reflecting on her life, the acerbic Betsy said, "Once I had every thing but money, now I have nothing but money." She also contended, "Had I waited, with my beauty and wit, I would have married an English Duke, instead of which I married a Corsican blackguard." As far as the people of Lewes were concerned, the young Baltimore beauty got everything that she deserved.

## You Look Out for the Spars

On Friday afternoon, May 25, 1798, Lewes was still buzzing about the Wiley-Wilson affair when the HMS *De Braak* shortened sail to take on a pilot. The pilot boat *Friendship* approached the British brig, and Andrew Allen prepared to board the *De Braak*. Aboard the British warship, Captain James Drew was in a jovial mood, and when Allen arrived aboard, Drew proclaimed, "I've had good luck."

The future captain of the *De Braak* was born on April 19, 1751, in the English village of Saltash near the port of Plymouth. When he was thirteen years old, Drew enlisted aboard the seventy-gun ship *Buford* as a captain's servant; and on the eve of the American Revolution, Drew had risen to first lieutenant aboard the sloop HMS *Scorpion*, part of the British squadron stationed at Boston. On June 17, 1775, the British decided to clear the colonists from the heights around Boston in what became known as the battle of Bunker Hill. Scorning a flank attack, the British attempted a frontal assault, and twice, they were repulsed. When the redcoats advanced a third time, the Americans were driven from the hill, but the English had suffered frightful casualties.

When the Americans abandoned their position, the patriots left many of their dead and wounded on the battlefield. Among the dead was the respected colonial leader Dr. Joseph Warren. After the fighting was over, James Drew and others inspected the colonial lines, and shortly afterward, reports reached the Americans that the battlefield visitors had committed atrocities on the dead and dying.

John Adams was a member of a committee that investigated these allegations, and he received a letter that claimed Drew picked his way through the dead corpses that littered the battlefield. When he discovered an American who was still alive, Drew shot him through the head. In addition, a day or two after the battle, Drew went to that part of the field where many of the Americans had been buried. When he happened upon the shallow grave of Dr. Warren, Drew dug into the earth until he located the American leader's corpse. Drew spit in Warren's face, stomped on the corpse and decapitated the body.

The incident did not appear to affect Drew's career in the British navy, and by the time Drew and the *De Braak* arrived off Cape Henlopen in May 1798, the atrocities at Bunker Hill had been forgotten. Drew's ship had originally been a Dutch vessel that was built in 1781 as a single-masted cutter. In 1795, the *De Braak* was captured by the English and rerigged with an additional mast. After the conversion, Captain Drew took command of the brig, and he complained that the ship was overmasted.

In 1798, when the *De Braak* arrived off Cape Henlopen, the exuberant Drew had completed a successful voyage, during which he had captured a Spanish merchant ship, the *Don Francisco Xavier*, laden with cargo of copper, cocoa and other goods. The captured Spanish vessel rode quietly on the waves a short distance from the *De Braak* as pilot Allen boarded the British brig, and Captain Drew proclaimed his good luck. Captain Drew planned to take on a supply of fresh water at Lewes, but at the moment, he was more interested in toasting his successful voyage and retreated to his cabin to fetch suitable drinks.

Allen, however, was concerned about the large black clouds that were rolling in from the west. While Drew was in his cabin rummaging through his liquor cabinet, Allen ordered the sails on the *De Braak* taken in. Drew returned a few minutes later and was furious. The British captain cursed at Allen and ordered the sails reset. Drew snapped at Allen, "You look out for the bottom, and I'll look out for the spars."

Andrew Allen understood that his principal job was to watch out for the ship's bottom by guiding the *De Braak* past the shoals and shallows that dotted the waters around Cape Henlopen. The pilot also knew that a sailing ship's delicate balance could be quickly upset by the Delaware coast's fickle weather.

After Drew's sharp exchange with Allen and his order to reset the sails, almost immediately, the squall that had been brewing over Rehoboth Bay slammed into the *De Braak*. The sudden wind filled the sheets, and the force tipped the *De Braak* to one side. In heavy weather, hatches and other deck openings would be covered with canvas and secured with battens to prevent water from flowing down to the lower decks. But when the *De Braak* arrived at Cape Henlopen, the weather was clear, and the hatches had not been battened down. When the squall forced the top-heavy vessel on its side, the ocean began to cascade across the deck, down the open hatches and into the hold of the British brig. Aboard the *De Braak*, the vessel's sharp shift sent some of the brig's contents careening to the low side of the ship, and this shift in weight made it more difficult for the brig to right itself.

Within seconds, many aboard the *De Braak* realized that the vessel was doomed. Some of the sailors were able to get into a small boat that was next to the brig. Others swam the short distance to the beach. Those who were below decks had to fight against the water that gushed down the ladders as the trapped sailors attempted to reach safety. In addition, the network of spars, sails and rigging ensnared some of those who had managed to escape the inside of the hull. A few minutes after the spring storm had struck, the *De Braak*'s hull settled on the sea floor. The water's surface was covered with debris that some sailors used as improvised rafts. Amid the flotsam, the upper ends of the *De Braak*'s masts stood silently above the waves.

Over half of those aboard the *De Braak* did not survive the disaster. Captain Drew was among the forty-seven British sailors and Spanish prisoners who were lost. Pilot Allen was only a few feet from Drew when the storm struck, and he broke his leg in the sudden lurching of the British brig. Despite his injury, Allen managed to avoid entrapment in the ship's rigging and was saved. When Allen reached safety, the Delaware pilot could honestly say, "I've had good luck."

According to tradition, there were several people on shore who watched in astonishment as the capsized warship slipped beneath the waves. Gilbert McCracken was among those who rushed to the beach, where he spotted three men clinging to a chest. As the surf carried the three sailors to the beach, McCracken helped them to dry land. When the three men had recovered from their brush with death, McCracken led them across the dunes to his home in Lewes.

After *De Braak* had settled to the ocean floor, the vessel's masts protruded above the waves. The location of the sunken brig was obvious to anyone walking the sands of Cape Henlopen, and the British made several attempts to salvage the warship. When these efforts failed, the wind and waves eventually carried away *De Braak*'s upper rigging, and all indications of the sunken vessel disappeared. In 1805, Gilbert McCracken and his son, Henry, went for a stroll near Cape Henlopen. As they walked, the conversation between fourteen-year-old Henry and his father turned to the sinking of HMS *De Braak*, the three survivors that the elder McCracken had helped and the tales of the gold and silver among the brig's captured cargo. Gilbert, an experienced bay pilot who knew a thing or two about navigation, stopped and took sightings of where the British brig sank. The tales of the treasure that the British ship carried passed into Lewes lore, and the residents never tired of regaling visitors with the stories of riches that could be found just off the Cape Henlopen beach.

Grave marker of Captain James Drew of the *De Braak* in St. Peter's churchyard on Second Street. *Photo by Michael Morgan.*

## BOMBS BURSTING IN AIR

When Jacob Jones left Ryves Holt's old house to join the U.S. Navy, he was one of the oldest midshipmen in the service. The thirty-one-year-old Jones was nearly twice the age of his fellow midshipmen, many of whom were still teenagers, but the prospect of a change in scenery may have been an inducement Jones couldn't deny. Jacob's mother died when he was an infant. After his mother's death, Jacob's father married Penelope Holt, the granddaughter of Ryves Holt of Lewes, but soon afterward, Jacob's father died. Penelope raised Jacob in Lewes, where he attended the academy and studied under Reverend Matthew Wilson.

At the age of eighteen, Jones left Lewes to study medicine under Dr. James Sykes of Dover. With his education completed, Jones moved back to the Ryves Holt House and began his medical practice, but few patients appeared. After his wife died, however, the Lewes resident decided to join the navy, and in 1798, the year the *De Braak* went down, Jones became a midshipman.

At the beginning of the nineteenth century, the pirates of Tripoli were raiding American merchant ships in the Mediterranean, and Jones was assigned to the frigate *Philadelphia*, which was ordered to the coast of North Africa. While cruising off Tripoli, the *Philadelphia* ran aground on a sandbar. Jacob Jones and the rest of the American crew were captured, and they spent the next two years in a Tripolitan prison.

Captain Jacob Jones was raised in Lewes and lived in the Ryves Holt House. He became a respected commander in the U.S. Navy. *Courtesy of the Delaware Public Archives.*

After his release, Jones continued his naval career, and in the early months of the War of 1812, he was in command of the eighteen-gun sloop *Wasp* when it sailed past Lewes and into the Atlantic. As he cruised southward, Jones encountered the British brig *Frolic*. After a brisk battle, the British ship surrendered. The victory seemed to signal a change in the luck of Jacob Jones, but before he could return to port, Jones encountered a large British squadron and was captured. Despite his numerous misfortunes, Jacob Jones was an excellent naval officer, and he continued to serve in various capacities in a career that lasted over half a century.

While Jones and the rest of the U.S. Navy were fighting the British at sea, the War of 1812 again put

Lewes on the front line with Colonel Samuel B. Davis as the commander of the forces defending the town. Davis, who was born in Lewes on December 25, 1765, went to sea as a young boy. By the time that he was an adult, he was a veteran sailor. In the course of his travels, Davis landed in New Orleans, where he met the merchant Daniel Clark, one of the richest men in America. Clark and Davis became business associates and close friends. Clark had a daughter, Myra, and shortly after she was born, Clark asked Davis to care for her. The Lewes native and his wife, Marian, believed that the arrangement was only temporary, but when Clark showed little interest in raising his daughter, Davis and his wife adopted Myra as their own child. When Davis moved into Henry Fisher's former house on Pilottown Road to oversee the defenses of Lewes, Myra played in the yard and swung on the fence gate near the creek.

On March 16, 1813, Davis led a contingent of Delaware troops across Lewes Beach to meet with a delegation of British officers from a powerful British flotilla anchored near Cape Henlopen. The enemy ships were under the command of Commodore James Beresford of the seventy-four-gun warship *Poiciters*, but the British warships were short of provisions. With the British warships anchored in full view of the town, Beresford dispatched a small boat with several officers aboard under a flag of truce.

When the officers reached Colonel Davis, they presented him with an ultimatum from Commodore James Beresford: "As soon as you receive this, I must request you will send twenty live bullocks, with a proportionate quantity of vegetables and hay, to the *Poitiers*, for the use of his Britannic Majesty's Squadron, now at this anchorage, which shall be immediately paid for at the Philadelphia prices. If you refuse to comply with this request, I shall be under the necessity of destroying your town." Having delivered the ultimatum, the British officers returned to their ships.

As soon as the people of southern Delaware learned of the British threat to destroy Lewes, volunteers flooded into town to defend it. Within days, over one thousand troops had assembled in Lewes. The old fortifications at the west end of Pilottown Road were reinforced with logs, earth, sand and gravel to create a rudimentary fort. A small watchtower added an impressive note to the earthworks. Close to the center of town, the defenders of Lewes built a second defensive work. In addition, defensive works were thrown up west of town near Block House Pond, which had acquired its name in the seventeenth century when the people of Lewes built a blockhouse nearby to defend the town's western approaches.

Beresford did little to improve the British fleet for an attack on the Delaware town. He already had weapons more powerful than any that the troops under Davis possessed. Nevertheless, the British commander waited three weeks for his demand to be met while he attempted to secure the needed supplies by raiding coastal farmhouses. During this time, several British officers went ashore at Cape May, where they were entertained at a New Jersey tavern with "every species of debauchery."

The residents of the Delaware town knew that they had survived the British navy during the American Revolution, and they were confident that they could do it again. One observer compared the reaction of the defenders of Lewes to the scorched-earth policy that greeted Napoleon Bonaparte's invasion of Russia: "[If] the enemy in our bay want bullocks, they should have them on terms which the Russians gave Bony Moscow."

As Beresford waited for a reply to his demand, the people of Lewes prepared to defend the town. To make it difficult for the British ships to maneuver, the lamps in the Cape Henlopen Lighthouse were ordered extinguished, and the buoy markers in the bay were shifted. In addition, men from Sussex County began to arrive in Lewes. One confident Delaware defender suggested:

> *We have about 1,000 citizen residing on the banks of our River and creeks who live by fishing, fowling and muskrat catching—put those useful men up, furnish them with suitable shot, embody them in classes of seven to every class, appoint a leader and rallying point, give them a handsome sum for every boot they destroy or capture belonging to the enemy, and good reward for every prisoner they take dead or alive.*

On April 6, 1813, the British flotilla assembled off Lewes, and the British fired two shots over the town to get the attention of the town's defenders. Several officers were sent ashore under a flag of truce, and they repeated Beresford's ultimatum: provide supplies or face destruction. Colonel Davis refused to comply. The British answered with a directive to evacuate the women and children, and a short time later, the bombardment of Lewes began. In his diary, Daniel Rodney of Lewes noted the first day of the attack: "The cannonade then commenced and continued till 10—their shot pitched beyond the town and did but little Damage—firing ceased until day light."

All the British warships were capable of firing solid shot that weighed up to thirty-two pounds apiece. These solid iron cannon balls could smash through the walls of the strongest building in Lewes. In addition, some of the British ships were armed with mortars that could lob exploding shells

Colonel Samuel Boyer Davis commanded the defenses of Lewes during the British bombardment in the War of 1812. *Courtesy of the Delaware Public Archives.*

into the Delaware town. The explosion from a mortar "bomb" could demolish most structures in Lewes. Finally, the British fired a number of Congreve rockets during the bombardment. These newly developed weapons were shaped like oversized skyrockets, with a cylinder several feet long and about six inches in diameter attached to a long pole. The cylinder was filled with black powder that served as a propellant. Attached to the end of the cylinder was an explosive or an incendiary device designed to start fires or used for illumination during night battles. The rocket could also be equipped with an iron shell that, when exploded, would send deadly scraps of metal flying.

On Wednesday, April 7, the British resumed the bombardment of Lewes with these fearsome weapons. In his diary, Rodney noted that "again began and continued [to] 5 or 6 last night. The firing of Bombs 12, 18, & 32 shot and Rockets till 1 o'clock in which time 537 shot were sent against the Town."

Although the sound and fury of the bombardment had been awesome, the results had been negligible. Many shots passed over the buildings and landed harmlessly in the fields beyond the town. The British solid shot hit a number of chimneys, knocked corner posts off several houses and lodged in the walls of buildings. Peter Hall's tavern was hit several times, and the building sustained significant damage. At one point, a woman heard a whistling sound over her head. She turned to her husband and asked, "What's that noise?" Her husband curtly answered, "Bullets, my dear."

During the bombardment of Lewes, most of the town's defenders huddled behind the breastworks of pine logs that had been erected along the creek. At Block House Pond, a number of the town's residents had taken shelter in

Some of the cannons that defended Lewes from the British attack as they appeared a century ago. *Courtesy of the Delaware Public Archives.*

the small fortification, including a pregnant woman who gave birth during the attack. The infant girl was cradled in a bed of corn stalks and lullabied by the boom of cannon.

Whenever possible, the Delaware troops fired back at the British, but the Americans were unable to damage the enemy ships. Colonel Davis decided on a bit of trickery to convince the British that a large army was defending the Delaware town. Davis ordered the militia and volunteers to march along the waterfront so that they could be seen by those aboard the British ships. Once the troops reached a point where the buildings shielded the troops from British view, the soldiers marched out of town. From there, they circled around to their original starting point. The result was a continuous parade of troops that appeared to be a vast army marching into Lewes.

When the bombardment was over, a few buildings had sustained minor damage, and a frustrated Beresford ordered the British squadron to set sail. The relieved residents of Lewes began to retrieve the debris of the shot and shell that littered the town. Rodney noted that "above 300 cannon balls besides bombs & rockets were picked up in town since the cannonade." A small shot that lodged in the foundation of a building on Front Street earned the building the nickname "Cannonball House." A Baltimore newspaper carried a dispatch from one of the defenders: "Our brave citizens being short of cannon-balls, the enemy was so

The Cannonball House before it was restored and turned into a museum. The cannonball is lodged in the large dark square in the foundation of the building. *Courtesy of the Delaware Public Archives.*

accommodating as to fire eight hundred on shore, which on picking up and finding they suited the caliber of our cannon remarkably well, the loan was immediately returned with *interest.*"

Another newspaper reported:

> *Commodore Beresford would seem to have suddenly altered his mind with respect to burning down Lewiston, to make a fire to roast the Delaware oxen by. It would be too offensive to suppose a British officer would threaten without meaning to make good his word…Delaware beef is highly seasoned, and if served up with forced meat balls, might not prove as palatable to this nautical hero as the beef of old England.*

On April 24, the *Niles Register* reported that, after the attack on Lewes, the British sought provisions from an easier prey: "We have nothing new from this quarter except that Sir John Beresford has captured five oyster-boats, and after a severe engagement, caused these whole cargoes to be devoured." The paper also described the results of the attack on the Delaware town:

"The people of Lewistown are making themselves quite merry for the late bombardment of that place. They enumerate their killed and wounded as follows: one chicken killed, one pig wounded—leg broken."

A year after the failed bombardment at Lewes, on August 24, 1814, the British routed an American army at Bladensburg, Maryland, and marched into Washington, D.C., where they burned the White House and other buildings. The British fleet headed for Baltimore, which they considered a "nest of pirates," vowing to also leave that city in flames. Baltimore was defended by Fort McHenry, which the British attacked with the same array of solid shot, mortars and rockets that they used at Lewes. While the British bombarded Fort McHenry on September 13 and 14, 1814, Francis Scott Key, an American lawyer who had gone to the English to secure the release of an American doctor, witnessed the attack from a British ship. Around dawn, when the bombardment was slackening off, the defenders of Fort McHenry raised a large thirty- by forty-two-foot American flag. Seeing the flag and concluding that the British attack had failed, Key was inspired to pen the lines to a poem that described the bombs bursting in air, the red glare of the rockets and the sight of the big American flag flying in the morning light. Key's poem was published under the title "The Defense of Fort McHenry," but soon it was universally known as "The Star Spangled Banner," containing the immortal phrase "land of the free and home of the brave." In contrast, some nameless wit summed up the attack on Lewes a year earlier in less inspiring words: "The commodore and his men, shot a pig and killed a hen."

## WHEN YOU GO

No other event is more visible today than the attack on Lewes by the British in 1813. In an article for *Harper's Monthly* in 1879, Pyle pointed out that "[Lewes] possesses, among many points of interest, an old fort built in 1812 for the defense of the town, which is still in a perfect state of preservation, with guns mounted precisely as they originally were." Although the cannons in Memorial Park next to the canal sit near colorful flowers and neat shrubs and may not be "mounted precisely as they originally were," these relics serve as visible reminders of Lewes's finest hour. Diagonally across the street is the Cannon Ball House, which has a piece of British ordinance embedded in its foundation, operated as a museum by the Lewes Historical Society.

A modern view of Blockhouse Pond where civilians sought refuge during the British bombardment. *Photo by Michael Morgan.*

Today, the cannons in Memorial Park sit on concrete bases amid colorful flowers. The building in the left background is the Cannonball House. *Photo by Michael Morgan.*

The sinking of the *De Braak* in 1798 spawned incredible stories that the vessel was laden with a cargo of gold, silver and other treasure. When the remains of the *De Braak* were located in 1986, the salvagers used heavy equipment to wrest the ship's timbers from the bottom of the bay.

Although a large number of century artifacts were recovered from the wreck of the *De Braak*, the heavy-handed recovery effort destroyed much of the archaeological evidence. The noted maritime historian Donald Shomette compared the recovery of the British warship to bulldozing Gettysburg. The timbers of the *De Braak* are in a small building in Cape Henlopen State Park, where they are sprayed with water to help preserve them.

A diver working in 1985 on the salvage of the *De Braak. Courtesy of the Delaware Public Archives.*

*Opposite, top*: The Cannonball House is now a museum operated by the Lewes Historical Society. *Photo by Michael Morgan.*

*Opposite, bottom*: The cannonball embedded in the foundation of the Cannonball House. *Photo by Michael Morgan.*

The lower timbers of the *De Braak* are in a small building on the grounds of Cape Henlopen State Park, where they are kept wet to prevent deterioration. *Photo by Michael Morgan.*

A ceramic bowl from the *De Braak* on display at the Zwaanendael Museum. *Photo by Michael Morgan.*

In 2004, a dredging project near the Roosevelt Inlet deposited a number of eighteenth-century artifacts on Lewes Beach. An archaeological investigation located a shipwreck in the inlet and identified it as the merchant ship *Severn*, which sank in 1774. The artifacts from the *Severn* have yielded a wealth of information about trade on the eve of the American Revolution. Some of the artifacts from the *De Braak* and *Severn* are on display in the Zwaanendael Museum on King's Highway at Savannah Road. The museum showcases the maritime, military and social history of Lewes. The remains of the *Severn* remain underwater near the inlet until time, money and technique are available to continue their systematic archaeological study.

# Chapter 4

# ON THE BEACH

## A VERY LARGE AND COMMODIOUS BUILDING

The failed British bombardment of Lewes left the town's estimated 140 houses relatively unscathed. The town had spread beyond Third Street down Ship Carpenter, Mulberry and Market Streets toward the banks of Block House Pond to accommodate a population of around one thousand residents. With the end of the War of 1812, Lewes residents returned to peaceful maritime pursuits, and as always, there was a concern about safely navigating the difficult waters around Cape Henlopen. In 1826, a report to Congress documented over 150 vessels that had been wrecked near the entrance to Delaware Bay between 1807 and 1826. The report helped to garner support for the construction of a breakwater near Cape Henlopen, and in 1828, Congress appropriated money to begin work.

Although large artificial breakwaters had been built in Europe, none had been constructed in America. The ambitious design called for two formidable stone barriers. A 3,600-foot breakwater that began several hundred feet from the beach and extended westward into the bay was intended to shelter ships from the stormy Atlantic. The second barrier was constructed on an angle over 1,300 feet from the western end of the breakwater. This smaller structure was designed to intercept ice flows from the upper reaches of the Delaware Bay and was known as the "icebreaker." Together, these two barriers were designed to provide a safe anchorage with calm, ice-free waters for the hundreds of vessels that sailed coastal waters.

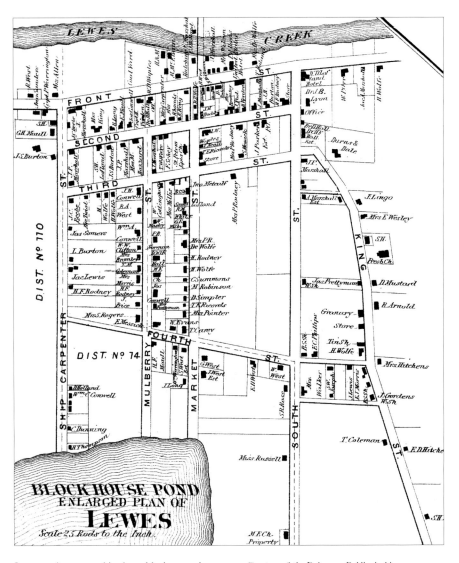

Lewes as it appeared in the mid-nineteenth century. *Courtesy of the Delaware Public Archives.*

The breakwater and the icebreaker were built using rubble mound construction by placing stones along the bay bottom in a line that was 160 feet wide at its base and tapered at a nearly forty-five-degree angle to a crest that was 14 feet above water and 22 feet wide. Using sailing vessels to transport the stone from quarries mostly along the Delaware River, the workers used simple levers, skids and pulleys (techniques that dated back to

The breakwater as depicted on an early twentieth-century postcard. *Courtesy of the Delaware Public Archives.*

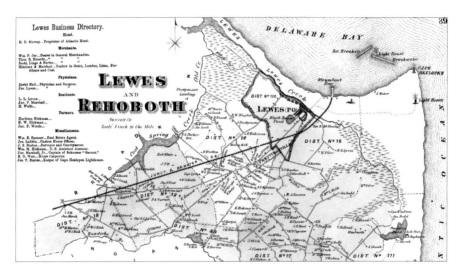

On this map, the railroad and the breakwater, two major nineteenth-century projects that impacted Lewes, are clearly shown. *Courtesy of the Delaware Public Archives.*

the construction of the pyramids) to muscle the stones, weighing between five hundred pounds to six tons, into place.

Work on the breakwater project was suspended for the winter in February 1831, when a massive storm drove two schooners and several pilot boats ashore on Lewes Beach. Although Lewes Creek normally afforded vessels some protection against high water and pounding waves, the 1831 storm was so fierce that the *Connecticut Courant* reported:

> *The tide in Lewes Creek was said to be four feet higher than ever was known before. The packet sloop,* Breakwater, *stern went into Richard's tavern house, and her main boom about six foot into his kitchen. The sloop* Josephine *was on the wharf and stove in the under pinning of Mr. Rodney's granary. The bridge across Lewes Creek gave way and all the wharves are gone.*

Fortunately, the winter storm did not affect work on the breakwater, and by 1840, the project was essentially finished. The breakwater and icebreaker were below their designed height and periodic construction continued for the next several decades until 1869, when the project was considered finished.

The completed breakwater fell over one thousand feet short of its projected length, but during the 1830s, when construction was underway, vessels began seeking shelter behind the unfinished barrier. In 1839, on average of fifteen vessels a day were sheltered behind the breakwater. Improvements to the Delaware Breakwater were made periodically for the rest of the nineteenth century, and during the first years of the twentieth century, a new breakwater was constructed east of the first stone barrier. In addition, various small lighthouses were built to warn approaching mariners of the stone barrier. The East End Light on the breakwater was painted a distinctive muted red color and became a symbol for Lewes.

Construction vessels lay stones on the bottom of Delaware Bay for the breakwater. *Courtesy of the Lewes Historical Society.*

When work began on the first breakwater, the Great Dune on Cape Henlopen was securely anchored in place. Writing for *Scribner's Magazine* in the late nineteenth century, John R. Spears reported:

> *According to gray-haired observers living near Henlopen, the sand wave…was fifty years ago, simply a great dune or ridge lying along the northerly side of the cape. The foot was washed by the waves whenever a northeast gale was blowing; its crown covered with twisted pines interspersed with patches of coarse grass.*

Soon after workers started laying stone in place for the breakwater, however, residents of Lewes noticed a change in the sand ridge. Northerly winds created dense storms that lifted clouds of coarse sand from the northern face of the ridge up and over the crest. The lighthouse keeper, beachcombers and others who ventured onto the dune during one of these gales covered their faces with handkerchiefs to avoid the choking sand. Wind drove the sand across the top of the ridge and deposited it in the lee of the dune. Trees that had thrived in the low ground on the landward side of the ridge were inundated by a flood of wind-blown sand.

The moving sand appears to be a slow-moving ocean wave as it inundates the pine forest of Cape Henlopen. *Courtesy of the Delaware Public Archives.*

The dune had been stirred to life by an apparent minor mishap. Men working on the breakwater came ashore and started a small campfire on the cape. The flames got out of control and spread quickly across the northern face of the high dune, consuming nearly all the trees and other vegetation in their path. Freed from the clutches of the roots that had held the sand in place for centuries, the liberated dune began to move. Nicknamed the "Walking Dune" of Cape Henlopen, the sand ridge traveled as much as sixty feet a year as it shifted inland.

The remarkable movement of the Great Dune and the construction of the breakwater were not the only changes taking place in and around Lewes during the nineteenth century. In 1847, *Blue Hen's Chicken*, a weekly Delaware newspaper that reported on developments throughout the state, noted that fishing was "admirable" in the waters behind the breakwater and the surrounding territory made for excellent hunting. Cape May had already established a brisk vacation trade, but according to the *Blue Hen's Chicken*:

> *The very large and commodious building called "Ocean House," erected by Mr. Solomon Prettyman and kept by his brother during the season, has been crowded with visitors, and done a very large business. We understand that it is contemplated to erect two or three other houses, and wharf by next season, as it is found that Cape Henlopen present as good a bathing ground and as many attractions as Cape May.*

Four years later, one of Prettyman's guests wrote:

> *A week's residence here, for the advantage of a change of atmosphere, sea bathing, &c., enables me to speak with certainty of its superiority as a temporary residence during the warm weather. Lewestown and Pilotstown are pleasant villages and contain within their borders much that is worthy…The location, at the southern point of the great Delaware Bay, is beautiful and commanding. Pleasant drives in all directions and along the seashore at low tide, or a gallop on horseback, a bath in the gentle surf of the bay, or the more boisterous surge of the Atlantic…I am a guest at the Ocean House, kept by the Messrs. Prettyman. It is a well arranged, admirable hotel, a quiet and orderly house.*

Three years after the Ocean House opened, the *Blue Hen Chicken* reported that Prettyman's hotel was frequented by vacationers from Delaware,

Victorian vacationers enjoy the shady porch of the Ocean House at Lewes Beach. *Courtesy of the Delaware Public Archives.*

Maryland, Pennsylvania and New Jersey. The hotel's rooms were large, airy and comfortable. In addition,

> *the bathing ground is delightful and the society of the ancient town of Lewes and neighborhood is excellent, celebrated in all time for its intelligence and hospitably. It will not be so much crowded as Cape May, and on that account more agreeable to many persons. The fishing and gunning can scarcely be excelled.*

Vacationers at the Lewes hotels spent time at the beach enjoying a "bath" (as swimming would not be popular for several decades), and they watched the steady parade of ships passing around Cape Henlopen. In addition to vessels engaged in the coastal trade, many fishing boats frequented the waters behind the breakwater. In 1853, a fleet of over fifty fishing vessels from New England sailed into the bay. The fishermen had been working the waters off the coast for several weeks when they decided to take a respite from their work and go ashore. After anchoring their boats behind the breakwater, the fishermen landed on the beach and marched across the bridge into Lewes, where they raised a considerable ruckus.

At first, the invasion seemed to be little more than a bunch of rowdy fishermen blowing off steam after several weeks at sea. After a day of

Vacationers once considered a dip in the bay waters of Lewes Beach a "bath." *Courtesy of the Delaware Public Archives.*

raucous behavior, the New Englanders left Lewes, went back to their boats and sailed out into the bay. Frustrated by their inability to find any fish, they sailed back to Lewes, where the *Delaware State Reporter* noted, "Angered and vexed with their disappointment, a large body of the men marched up to the town, where they committed the most excessive acts of riotous behavior. They made forcible entrances into private dwellings, frightening and insulting the female occupants. A few energetic individuals succeeded in driving them back to their boats and the town authorities forbade them from returning at their peril."

Having been invaded twice by the riotous fishermen, the people of Lewes were determined not to let them return. When a report reached the town that over 150 fishermen bent on attacking the town were crossing the beach, the people of Lewes armed with themselves with guns, muskets and clubs. The mob of fishermen would have to cross Lewes Creek to reach the town, and residents of Lewes gathered on the town's side of the bridge to prevent them from doing so. Undeterred by the sight of the armed townsfolk, the fishermen attempted to force their way across the creek and into Lewes. The result was a mêlée during which heads were bloodied and bones were broken. An old cannon was rolled up to the bridge and loaded with small scraps of iron. The cannon was fired into the milling mob of New Englanders, who beat a hasty retreat to the beach, where they boarded their boats and sailed away. The fishermen, like the British navy before them, had learned that the residents of Lewes were formidable foes when they were driven to defend their town.

## When the Atlantic Howls

Eight years after Lewes repulsed the attack of the New Jersey fishermen, the Civil War began, and once again, Lewes came under attack by a boatload of ruffians. Although Delaware was a slave state, it was the first state to ratify the federal Constitution, and its residents were firmly devoted to the Union; but in July 1861, a group of Southern sympathizers aboard a steamer docked at Lewes. The secessionists marched into town, where they defiantly made their support for the Confederacy known, and toward evening, they were reinforced with a number of armed comrades. After assembling on the creek bank, the rowdy crowd, now well oiled with alcohol, began to march into Lewes, where an armed group of Union-supporting sailors had assembled. The sailors had an old six-pounder cannon, and when the Southerners came into range, they spotted the cannon, sobering the Southerners, who retreated to their steamer and sailed away. The old cannon became a symbol of Union support, and it was fired to celebrate Northern victories. Late in the war, secessionists grew weary of the booming cannon, and they stole the antiquated artillery piece, which they buried on a farm on Pilottown Road.

When President Abraham Lincoln called for volunteers to suppress the Southern rebellion, white men from Lewes joined the Union army, and in 1863, when regiments composed of black soldiers were authorized, a number of African Americans from Lewes enlisted in the Northern forces. George H. Wright and Matthew Johnson enlisted in the Twenty-fifth Regiment of the U.S. Colored Troops (USCT). Not much is known about Wright and Johnson, but it was common for men from the same town to enlist together. They joined the regiment on the same day, and both were assigned to Company K. Wright, Johnson and the rest of the Twenty-fifth spent the rest of the war serving as reserves and on garrison duty, and during their service, they faced one of the greatest hazards to befall Civil War soldiers—disease. During the spring and summer of 1865, the regiment suffered from an epidemic of scurvy. At one point, an average of five men died daily from the disease, which was caused by poor rations. Although the officers of the regiment pleaded with their superiors to send fresh provisions, over 150 men died before sufficient food could be provided. At the end of the war, the regiment was disbanded, and the troops were discharged.

Following the Civil War, the return to peace saw growth in the number of sightseeing boats traveling from Wilmington and Philadelphia to Lewes. Joseph Leidy, a professor of anatomy at the University of Pennsylvania, took an excursion boat from Philadelphia to Lewes. As the vessel neared Lewes, several passengers spotted the shell mounds along the beach and began debating their origins. Leidy turned to the vessel's captain, "Skipper, what's your guess about it?" The captain gruffly answered, "Well, Doc, our folks always said that they was Indian heaps, but we don't pay them no attention." Leidy continued to study the mounds and quietly replied, "My, my."

When the vessel docked at Lewes, Leidy hiked over to the mounds and used a stick to poke into the shells. Very quickly, Leidy uncovered pieces of pottery, arrowheads and other Native American artifacts. When he returned to the University of Pennsylvania, Leidy shared his discoveries with his colleagues, and his findings initiated scholarly interest in the early inhabitants of the Cape Henlopen region. Although Leidy's report on the objects that he had discovered helped launched archaeology in Delaware, the shell mounds continued to lie at the mercy of the elements. In a few more decades, development of Lewes Beach and the continued movement of the sands of Cape Henlopen would eradicate the shell mounds that were once one of the coast's most distinctive man-made features.

The end of the Civil War enabled railroad construction in Delaware to resume, and in 1869, the Junction and Breakwater Railroad was completed to Lewes. A short time later, a spur was built to Cape Henlopen to serve the growing activity on the bay beach. This spur, known as the Lewes Beach Track, ran to the east of town and brought a boost to Lewes as a vacation destination. The Ocean House reopened, and it was joined by other hotels on the beach, among them the Pavilion House near the railroad pier.

A postcard view of the Lewes train station. *Courtesy of the Delaware Public Archives.*

A steamboat, passengers and sightseers crowd the Transportation Pier at Lewes Beach in the early twentieth century. *Courtesy of the Delaware Public Archives.*

Following the Civil War, the U.S. Life-Saving Service was established by Congress, and a series of lifesaving stations, staffed by professional surfmen, were built along the coast. In 1876, the Cape Henlopen Life-Saving Station was opened near the ocean beach south of the lighthouse, and eight years later, the Lewes Station was completed on the bay beach.

The lifesaving stations were headed by "Keepers" who commanded a crew of a half dozen surfmen along quasi-military lines. The centerpiece of each lifesaving station was a surfboat, which was mounted on large wheels so that it could be rolled easily across the sand. When the boat was pushed into the waves, the surfmen expertly hopped aboard and took up the oars. If the storm was too strong to allow the use of the surfboat, surfmen used a Lyle gun to fire a line to the stranded ship, and a breeches buoy would be used to ferry those on the ship to the beach. When the weather was too severe to risk a ride in the open breeches buoy, stranded people were placed in an enclosed surf car and were pulled to the beach. As one nineteenth-century observer pointed out, "A principal reason for the efficiency of this service is that men who know the coast and its local navigation, its currents, eddies and bars—fishermen and surfmen—have been its agents. No 'amateurs' have been employed."

In early March 1888, several dozen vessels huddled behind the Delaware Breakwater as a blizzard swept over the Atlantic Coast. The storm-tossed ocean waves broke over the breakwater, crashed into the ships and tore several vessels from their anchors. When the storm eased the next day, two dozen vessels had been sunk or severely damaged. Those that were still afloat had their spars, rigging and upper decks encased in ice.

The boathouse from the Lewes Life-Saving Station now sits at Canalfront Park. *Photo by Michael Morgan.*

When day broke on the morning of March 12, John A. Clampitt, the keeper of the Lewes Station, mustered his crew and headed for the beach. The force of the gale was so great, however, that the sand and sleet whirling in their faces so cut and buffeted them that they were forced to lie on the ground and crawl on their hands and knees back to the station. Half an hour later, the weather lulled somewhat, and the surfmen again set forth, joined by Keeper Theodore Salmon and surfmen from the Cape Henlopen Station. A few hundred yards offshore, the schooner *Allie H. Belden* was fast aground with its crew clinging to the rigging.

After several attempts by the Lewes surfmen to use their Lyle gun to fire a line to the stranded schooner, Clampitt decided to launch the surfboat, but the winds were so strong that the surfmen manning the oars were quickly exhausted. After nine hours of grueling work in the icy storm, the surfmen reached the stricken schooner, where they rescued the *Allie H. Belden*'s captain, mate and two seamen, who had clung to the rigging, exposed to the snow and wind for twelve hours. Two other sailors had already died, but these four cold but alive men from the schooner were ferried ashore.

At two o'clock in the morning, Keeper Thomas Truxton, of the Rehoboth Beach Station, led his crew on a grueling march across six miles of storm-swept beach to arrive on the cape at first light. Truxton's surfmen joined

A three-masted schooner's crushed stern was among the vessels damaged by the 1888 winter storm. *Courtesy of the Delaware Public Archives.*

the crew of the Lewes station in an attempt to rescue the crew of a three-masted schooner stranded on a sandbar six hundred yards from the beach. The ice was so thick that a rescue boat could not be rowed to the schooner. Three attempts to use a Lyle gun to fire a line to the stranded vessel ended in failure; and it was decided to make a final effort with the boat. When the boat was slid onto the ice, Truxton had oars put down on each side of it as supports for the men. By sliding the boat and oars alternately forward, they were able to drag the boat to within fifty feet of the schooner. At this point, the ice was thinner, and it was too dangerous to push the boat any farther. One of the men tried to throw a line to the schooner, but it fell short. On seeing this, the crew of the schooner tossed a line that landed on the thin ice out of the reach of the surfmen.

At this point, Truxton laid two oars on the ice and used them to help support his weight as he crawled slowly toward the end of the line from the schooner. If he were to hit a soft spot in the ice, Truxton would be plunged into the frigid water with little chance of rescue. Nonetheless, the keeper slowly slid his way forward until he reached the end of the line. The ice was too thin for him to let go of the oars. Desperate to save those aboard the stranded vessel, Truxton grasped the line with his teeth and gradually made his way back to the surfmen and the rescue boat. With Truxton's rope stretched between the boat and the schooner, a second line was stretched between the boat and the shore. Although it was extremely difficult work, those on the beach were able to ferry the crewmen from the schooner safely ashore.

At daybreak on March 14, the weather had moderated, but a strong breeze continued to blow snow squalls across the bay, where nearly every craft in the harbor was now fast in the ice. As soon as it was light enough, the surfmen of the Lewes and Cape Henlopen Stations resumed rescue operations, and by March 15, four days after the storm had started, the last sailors were finally brought ashore. The Great White Hurricane, as the blizzard of 1888 was sometimes called, damaged or destroyed thirty-five vessels near Cape Henlopen.

Theodore Salmons was the keeper of the Cape Henlopen Life-Saving Station during the blizzard of 1888, and after three decades of service, in 1907, a dinner was held in his honor. W.E. Tunnell, superintendent of the Sixth Life-Saving District addressed the guests, and he could not restrain his praise for Keeper Salmons. After three decades of service, Tunnell told surfmen from the Lewes and Cape Henlopen Life-Saving Stations, "He has saved more lives from the sea than any other man in the Life-Saving Service." Although Tunnell failed to mention him, Salmons could not have done it without his horse, "Bob."

During the winter months, the surfmen braved the frigid temperatures and icy winds to maintain a careful watch on the Delaware coast. When the weather was pleasant, the keeper could take one day off per week, and he could allow each of his crew of surfmen the same privilege, as long as

Amid the damage, several men inspect a small boat on a sailing vessel after the 1888 winter storm. *Courtesy of the Delaware Public Archives.*

only one man was away at a time. Whenever he could, Salmons hitched up Bob and made the trip to Lewes. Bob and Salmons were companions, and they had a special bond that was forged from many years of sharing the hardships of the windblown trips to the station.

When Superintendent Tunnel spoke of Salmons's service, he did not mention Bob, but it did not matter. Bob would continue to serve Salmons in his retirement. Unfortunately, that did not last long. Eight months after the dinner celebrating his service, Keeper Salmons passed away, and Bob was inconsolable. He lay down in his stall and refused to eat or lift his head. Several veterinarians were called, but they could not do anything for him. When Bob passed away, the veterinarians declared that he had died of a broken heart, and he was buried near the lifesaving station that Salmons had served so well.

# I WILL DRINK YOUR BLOOD

The Life-Saving Service did admirable work rescuing mariners from storm-tossed ships in distress; but even on the calmest days, the Delaware Bay could be treacherous. When Henry Hudson sailed past Cape Henlopen in 1609, the explorer quickly discovered that Delaware Bay was punctuated by numerous shoals and sandbars that could wreck the stoutest ship. As Philadelphia grew into one of America's great ports, the need for pilots to guide ships past the shallows of the bay increased. Tradition has it that the first Delaware Bay pilots were Native Americans whose intimate knowledge of the sandbars and shallows of the bay enabled them to guide colonial sailing ships through the bay's treacherous waters. During the nineteenth century, there were so many pilots available that they had to compete for the right to guide a vessel up the bay. In order to greet ships before they reached the mouth of the bay, groups of pilots from Lewes banded together to buy fast-sailing schooners that they used to reach ships that were still miles from Cape Henlopen.

The pilot schooners cruised in the vicinity of Cape Henlopen watching for an approaching ship that might need a pilot. At sea for days at a time, the schooners were equipped with all the necessities, and a few of the luxuries, of life. The interiors of these sleek vessels were furnished like a railroad sleeping car. Rows of polished mahogany berths ran fore and aft between decks. To provide privacy, each cozy and comfortable berth was equipped with heavy brocade curtains and sliding doors. Next to the sleeping quarters was a dining room that was equipped with inviting revolving chairs that were secured to the cabin floor.

In the nineteenth century, there were eight pilot schooners with several pilots aboard that sailed out of Cape May and Lewes to meet inbound ships. Reaching a ship first was not an easy task during the sailing ship era. The schooners had to sail against the easterly winds that the captains of square-

Pilots would spend days at a time aboard small schooners like this one waiting for ships to guide up the bay. *Courtesy of the Lewes Historical Society.*

riggers sought to propel them toward Cape Henlopen. The pilot schooners' fore-and-aft rig, raked masts and slim hull enabled them to sail close to the wind as they tacked their way toward an incoming ship. Sometimes, these vessels cruised several hundred miles into the Atlantic to meet an approaching ship because the first pilot to board an incoming vessel would serve as its pilot for both the incoming and outbound trip. After the winning boat delivered a pilot safely aboard, the pilot boats returned to their routine of sailing back and forth across the mouth of the bay.

On November 22, 1884, the pilot schooner *Enoch Turley* rendezvoused with the steamship *Pennsylvania* off Cape Henlopen in the middle of a winter storm. The frigid temperatures, a strong gale and heavy seas did not deter pilot Thomas Marshall as he boarded the *Turley*'s skiff with fellow pilot Marshall Bertrand. Also in the small boat were Andreas Hansen and Alfred Swansen, apprentice pilots. Bertrand was a slightly built twenty-five-year-old young man, raised by his grandfather, William Marshall, a member of one of Lewes's illustrious pilot families.

The skiff navigated the high waves to the steamer and delivered Marshall safely to the *Pennsylvania*. On the return trip to the *Turley*, however, the small boat was battered by the towering waves, and Bertrand, Hansen and Swansen lost sight of the pilot boat. The crew of the *Turley* also could not see the small skiff amid the towering waves, and the unrelenting northwest wind drove the small boat farther and farther away from the Delaware coast. The sailors aboard the *Turley* signaled the other pilot boats about the lost skiff, and the schooners began a fruitless search of several hundred square miles of ocean.

Aboard the skiff, the three men attempted to row toward the lightships stationed off the coast, but the winds continued to blow them out to sea. After a frigid night with no provisions aboard the small boat, all three men were cold, thirsty and famished. The freezing spray coated the men with a thin film of ice as they continued bailing excess water from the bottom of the open boat. The skiff was drifting northward when Bertrand spotted a square-rigged sailing ship, which maintained a steady course toward the small boat, and the three frantic men began to shout. By this time, the ship was nearly on top of the small skiff. Bertrand and the two sailors could see the captain and the crew of the sailing ship as it slid effortlessly through the waves.

When it appeared to Bertrand that those aboard the ship were making no effort to stop, he stood up in the skiff and shouted, "Captain, in the name of God throw us some bread or give me a line!" Aboard the ship, the captain appeared to wave as he sailed by the desperate men. The despondent Bertrand muttered, "By God, I hope you'll sink before sunset."

Toward evening of the second day in the boat, the two apprentices became delirious and pitched the oars, the bailing bucket and everything else that was loose into the sea. Exhausted by their outburst, the two men calmed down for a while, but during the night, Swanson took out his knife and stared out Marshall. Hansen declared grimly, "I'm going to slit you open and drink your blood" and lunged at the pilot. Marshall was able to fend off the attack by Hansen, who collapsed in the bottom of the small skiff.

Wave-driven water continued to collect in the bottom of the boat, and Bertrand took off one of his boots to use as a bailer. As he worked, Swansen was roused from a deep sleep, and when Hansen failed to stir, the other two men realized that the sailor was dead. Though they were lost at sea with no food and no help in sight, the storm had abated, and if the two men could maintain some strength, there was hope that they would be rescued. Bertrand suggested the only course of action and Swansen agreed. The two men striped off Hansen's ice-coated garments, plunged their knives into his chest and drank the dead sailor's blood. After pausing for a moment from the detestable task, they then began to strip slices of flesh from Hansen's legs. Having eaten as much as they could, the two men lay down near the mutilated sailor's body and rested.

Every now and then, one of the men would get up to see if there were any vessels in the vicinity. When the sun came up on Wednesday morning, Bertrand spotted the three-masted schooner *Emma F. Angell* heading in the direction of the skiff. Waving a flag that he fashioned from his raingear and a stick, Bertrand failed to attract the attention of anyone on the schooner. As the sailing vessel passed the stranded men by, Bertrand dipped his hand into the ocean and used the seawater to wet his parched lips, and he let out the loudest cry that he had ever uttered.

Aboard the schooner, someone heard Bertrand's call for help and saw the small skiff bobbing on the waves. Captain Gustavus Tripp of the *Emma F. Angell* ordered the schooner to turn about. As Tripp maneuvered the schooner to pick up Bertrand and Hansen, the two lifted Swansen's mutilated body and slid it into the ocean. Swansen later said, "The body was so badly cut up that we didn't want anyone to see it."

When the schooner reached the small boat, Bertrand was able to climb up the schooner's ladder, but Swansen was so weak that he had to be hauled aboard by a rope. After the two men were rescued, Tripp set sail for Lewes, where Bertrand spent several months in the hospital recovering from his ordeal. Undeterred by the horrors that he faced at sea, Bertrand continued to work as a pilot for another forty years.

By the late nineteenth century, it was obvious that the Lewes pilots could no longer rely on schooners to carry them out to meet incoming ships. Small groups of pilots were able to finance the schooners, but steam-powered pilot boats were so expensive that a large organization was needed to own and operate them. In 1896, the Pilots' Association for the Bay and River Delaware was formed, and the organization ordered a $65,000 steamboat to replace the sailing schooners.

The first steam pilot boat, the *Philadelphia*, with a distinctive letter *P* painted on its smokestack, went into service in 1897; a year later, the United States went to war with Spain. The U.S. Navy needed a number of small vessels that could operate in the coastal waters off Cuba, and it bought the *Philadelphia* for $100,000, mounted a battery of rapid-fire Hotchkiss guns and renamed the gunboat the *Peoria*.

On the night of June 30, 1898, the *Peoria*, under the command of Lieutenant Thomas William Ryan, escorted two transports to the port of Tunas on the southern coast of Cuba. The transports carried a cargo of

The pilot boat *Philadelphia* that was powered by steam and greatly simplified the pilots' task of rendezvousing with ships needing a pilot. *Courtesy of the Lewes Historical Society.*

munitions, three hundred Cuban insurgents and a detachment of the Tenth U.S. Cavalry. As the transports steamed toward shore, they were discovered by the Spanish, who opened a brisk fire. The transports retreated, and in the process, one of them went aground. Fortunately, the American gunboat *Helena* happened upon the *Peoria* and the two transports, and the gunboat was able to pull the grounded vessel free. At this point, a man in a small boat was spotted rowing toward the small American squadron. According to the commander of the *Helena*, "During the night of the 30th a Cuban had pluckily made his way off to the *Peoria* in a canoe, at imminent risk of being shot for his pains." The Cuban advised the Americans that they could land the insurgents a short distance east of Tunas.

Two nights later, the *Peoria* and the *Helena* opened fire on the Spanish at Tunas. Meanwhile, the transports sailed a few miles to the east, where the troops and their supplies were safely landed. The incident at Tunas demonstrated the value of small, swift gunboats, and after the Spanish-American War, the *Peoria* continued to serve in the navy.

After the navy had purchased the *Philadelphia*, the Pilots' Association had a second vessel built for $70,000. The new pilot boat was also named the *Philadelphia*, and for half a century, it delivered pilots to inbound steamers so that on the last leg of their voyage, they could safely navigate the waters of Delaware Bay.

## WHEN YOU GO

Not much is known about the U.S. Colored Troops from Lewes who fought in the Civil War, except that George H. Wright and Matthew Johnson are buried in St. George's Cemetery on Pilottown Road. Their tombstones bear their names, ranks, regiment and the proud designation "U.S.C.T."

At the start of the nineteenth century, the Siconese shell mounds were as high as thirty feet and one hundred feet in diameter, but subsequent development and natural erosion has covered most traces of these monuments to the Native

The tombstone of Civil War veteran George Wright in St. George's Cemetery. *Photo by Michael Morgan.*

St. George's Cemetery on Pilottown Road is the final resting place of many of the early African American residents of Lewes. *Photo by Michael Morgan.*

American presence. A public beach, a station for the bay pilots, the facilities for the Lewes-Cape May Ferry and modern housing now line the bayfront.

The National Harbor of Refuge and Delaware Breakwater Historic District has been established to include the stone barriers and their lighthouses built in the nineteenth and early twentieth centuries. Since most of the stonework is hidden underwater, their appearance belies the enormous amount of work that went into the construction of what was one of the largest projects undertaken by the federal government.

# Chapter 5

# AT THE CAPE

## FEAR OF THE POX

In 1808, a ship sailed into Lewes Harbor carrying a sick sailor, suffering from chills, fever, nausea, aches and other flu-like symptoms. The sick seaman was brought ashore and treated, but he did not improve. The sailor developed a rash, and the worst fears of those attending the sick man were realized. The sailor had smallpox. An estimated 40 percent of those who contracted smallpox died, and those who recovered were left with numerous small scars that gave the disease its name.

In the early nineteenth century, the doctors of Lewes did not understand what caused smallpox, but they did know of a way to keep the disease from spreading. At that time, Delaware doctors prevented the spread of smallpox by inoculating healthy people with fluids drawn from an infected person. In most cases, the inoculated person contracted only a mild form of the disease from which he or she would recover. After those who had been inoculated were restored to health, they were immune to smallpox. Some people died from the smallpox inoculation, but the death rate was much lower than contracting the disease "the natural way."

In 1808, a reported five hundred people were vaccinated in Lewes, and only one person, Hanna Holland, who had vaccinated herself, contracted the disease. In most cases, however, the most effective means of preventing the spread of contagious diseases continued to be isolating the sick from the general population.

Nearly eight decades later, a small boat carrying James Atwald landed at Lewes, and the well-dressed Englishman picked up his luggage and quietly made his way into town. Avoiding as many of the town's residents as well as he could, Atwald, who walked with a slightly limp, took a room at a boardinghouse. When he arrived in Lewes in February 1883, the unusually blotchy colors of his skin blended together until his flesh appeared variegated with silver streaks running through it. The visible lumps on the Englishman's skin did not appear to give him any pain or inconvenience, but whenever Atwald rubbed his hands together, he created a small cloud of fine, bran-like dust. The Englishman's peculiar appearance fed rumors that he was afflicted with a serious disease, and when confronted by the people of Lewes, Atwald freely admitted that he had leprosy.

From ancient times, leprosy was misunderstood and feared. With no known cure, the stigmatized patients who contracted the disease were usually ostracized and forced to live in separate "leper" colonies. Before arriving in Lewes, Atwald believed he contracted the disease in Madagascar; and when he first realized that he had leprosy, he was so despondent that he considered committing suicide. Believing that colder weather mitigated the effects of the disease, Atwald decided to go to Canada, but when the captain of the ship on which he was traveling discovered his reclusive passenger had leprosy, he put Atwald ashore at Lewes, where the people fell back on a biblical treatment of those inflicted with leprosy. Atwald was summarily banished from the town. According to the *New York Times*, "The extravagant stories that went rapidly from mouth to mouth caused such agitation that a special meeting of the town council was decided upon to consider ways and means to rid the community of the dangerous patient."

Two years after Atwald arrived in Lewes, the Delaware Breakwater quarantine station was established at Cape Henlopen to intercept any immigrant bound for Philadelphia who showed symptoms of an infectious disease. During the nineteenth century, immigrant ships were often floating pestholes, and seasoned sailors could identify immigrant ships by their smell. At first, the station's hospital facilities were a modest six beds and a few workrooms, but eventually, the installation spread over forty-one acres on the dunes of the cape. Dr. William P. Orr, a native of Lewes and the assistant acting surgeon in the Marine Hospital Service, served as the Breakwater Hospital's first director. (Dr. Orr's great-great-grandfather was the William Orr who purchased some of Captain's Kidd's loot. William Penn had decreed that Orr be banished from the coastal area, but he remained in Lewes, and the family became a mainstay of the community.) In *A Small-*

*Town Boyhood in the First State*, Dr. Orr's son, Robert, recalled his father's work at the quarantine station:

> *His job was to check for contagion on incoming foreign ships which had to be cleared to Philadelphia. The crew were examined on their ships for contagious diseases and, if contagion was found, the crew members were sent ashore for treatment at the Quarantine Station. The station was located near where the public fishing pier now is. The Station boasted a full line of services including hospital, graveyard, crematoriums, etc.*

According to Robert, it was customary for the captain to give his father a gift for his work: "Dad refused alcoholic gifts; however, he once accepted a parrot, unaware that it had been exposed to the salty language of this three-masted schooner's crew. Upon being introduced to our household for several days, my mother demanded that this bird with such colorful language be expelled at once."

For the first ten years after the hospital opened in 1885, the facility operated on a seasonal basis. At that time, many sailing ships crossing the Atlantic Ocean avoided the stormy winter season. By 1895, nearly all sailing ships had been displaced by steamships, and the quarantine station was kept open all year. Immigrants who were suspected of carrying a contagious disease could be quarantined at the station for as little as ten days or as long as two months. With the number of immigrants flooding to America increasing every year, the hospital was expanded to accommodate the large number of travelers who failed the health inspection. A series of barracks buildings were constructed that could sleep 1,500 steerage-class passengers. A separate building that could house 150 passengers was built for the well heeled and healthier cabin-class travelers.

In addition to the accommodations for the quarantined passengers, the station contained a bathhouse, surgeons' quarters, a disinfecting house and several support buildings. In 1915, the Italian steamer *Verona* reached Cape Henlopen with several hundred immigrants. Many of the immigrants were eager to reach Philadelphia, where they hoped to spend Easter with friends and relatives. Their trip, however, was sidetracked. A suspected case of smallpox was reported aboard the *Verona*, and the immigrants were duly marched to the quarantine station for an extended stay.

A group of immigrants, tired of the delay, devised a plan to break out from the station. Two hundred immigrants forced their way through the wire fence that enclosed the grounds and brushed past the guards who were woefully unprepared for such a mass exodus. The immigrants headed for the railroad station, three miles away. At the station, the crowd demanded tickets for Philadelphia, but the agent, brandishing a pistol, refused to sell them. The standoff at the railroad station ended when the revenue cutter *Onondaga* arrived with a detachment of fifty marines with rifles and fixed bayonets. The unarmed immigrants abruptly retreated to the friendlier confines of the quarantine station. The next day, a steamer arrived to take the immigrants to Philadelphia, and the great escape came to a happy conclusion.

World War I curtailed the flow of immigrants across the Atlantic, and when the United States entered the war in 1917, the navy took over the grounds of the quarantine station. After the war ended, legislation was passed that restricted the number of immigrants allowed into the United States, and the quarantine station, which had processed 200,000 immigrants, was no longer needed. A few years later, the station was abandoned.

## CASE OF THE STINKING FISH

In the early seventeenth century, the sight of several whales near the mouth of the Delaware Bay convinced the Dutch leaders of the ill-fated Swanendael colony that a whale station on Cape Henlopen would be profitable. The Dutch settlers, however, found only a single carcass of a dead whale that had washed onto the beach. After the destruction of Swanendael, the residents of Lewes had little interest in hunting the great beasts of the ocean, but in the nineteenth century, they began to pursue a much smaller and plentiful fish: the lowly menhaden.

In 1607, Captain John Smith had encountered a school of menhaden so numerous that he tried to catch them with a frying pan. Several hundred thousand menhaden traveled in schools that were so large that they were sometimes mistaken for small islands, but for years, the oily and bony fish were ignored. The development of mechanized presses, however, provided an economical method for extracting oil from the fish. One thousand menhaden fielded about fourteen gallons of oil that was used in lamps, paint and other products.

Following the Civil War, S.S. Brown & Company and the Luce Brothers erected fish-processing factories on the beach between Lewes and Cape Henlopen, and the town became the homeport for a small fleet of fishing vessels. These small boats were not smart-looking yachts, but they were

Menhaden fishing boats, large and small, moored at a pier on Lewes Beach. *Courtesy of the Delaware Public Archives.*

among the fastest sailing crafts on the water. Most vessels in the menhaden fleet were about fifty feet long and eighteen feet wide. These durable boats carried a crew of eight to ten men who sailed from Lewes in fair and foul weather. The menhaden fishermen used seines that were seven hundred feet long and up to one hundred feet deep to corral their catch, which could amount to seventeen tons in a single boat.

After the fish were muscled aboard, the boats set sail for the Lewes fish factories, where the fish were boiled in large tanks of water. The water was then removed, and a hydraulic press was used to extract the oil and water from the fish. The water containing the oil extracted from the fish was collected in tanks, where the oil rose to the surface and could be skimmed off. Some of the oil, however, remained in the water; and this water was dumped into Delaware Bay.

The fermenting fish scraps provided food for masses of maggots that produced swarms of flies and an odor that was overpowering. A nineteenth-century observer remarked, "The fetid odors aris[es] from these works and permeat[e] the atmosphere for miles in their vicinity, making them a nuisance, so far as odor is concerned, to their neighborhoods." According to John A. Clampitt, the keeper of the Lewes Life-Saving Station, which was

Even with modern improvements, menhaden had to be muscled aboard by hand. *Courtesy of the Lewes Historical Society.*

located not far from the processing plants, "Sometimes I would be at the table, and I would get up from the table and come out and get a whiff of that odor and I would then lose my meal."

Fortunately for Clampitt and the surfmen of his lifesaving station, they were on duty during the fall and winter months when the menhaden season was mostly over. On the other hand, shortly after the fish-processing plants were erected, the government established the Marine Hospital and quarantine station less than one mile away. After these facilities became operational, they were immediately invaded by the odors from the fish factories. In addition, the swarms of flies that the factories spawned descended on the lifesaving station, Marine Hospital, quarantine station and everything else in the vicinity. The smell and flies were so intolerable that the government took the fish factories to court for operating a public nuisance.

The case was held in the Federal Circuit Court in Dover with District Judge Edward G. Bradford presiding. In addition to Clampitt, a parade of other witnesses testified on the repulsive odors and flies. Dr. William Orr was called from his duties at the quarantine station to provide even-handed

As this postcard shows, despite their foul odors, the menhaden processing plants remained a highlight of a visit to Lewes. *Courtesy of the Delaware Public Archives.*

testimony about the smell and insects. Orr said, "Whenever the wind would blow from the direction of the fish factories, I could smell the odor. There is no doubt in my mind that it came from the factories…Whenever the wind blows from the direction of the factories the flies are always very thick."

On the other hand, Orr's professional training led him to doubt the direct harm that was done to people. He testified, "I do not believe that they are injurious to health except to those people—and there are quite a number of them around Lewes—who are continually annoyed by the scent from the factories and the worry to which they are subjected by it." Orr went on to testify that the odor did no physical harm, but he believed that the residents of Lewes thought that the smells affected their health and "that there are people who are affected by it simply because they are annoyed so much by it."

Other doctors at the quarantine station were more emphatic about the harm done by the odors and flies. Dr. Henry D. Geddings, the commanding surgeon at the Marine Hospital, testified:

> *The annoyance from flies was a very serious one. They came from the decomposing fish and from the fish scrap into which these fish were converted. They were literally in swarms. The flies were so thick it became necessary to screen every window at the station, being over seventy in number, in the*

*buildings occupied, and the swarms of flies were so thick that they would cut off the view through these windows and screens.*

Dr. C.P. Wertenbaker, commanding the quarantine station in 1894, told the court that the flies and odors were a menace to public health and that "I think it would be far wiser for the government to confiscate and destroy, paying all damages, than to let them remain there. It would be cheaper, many times cheaper, in the end."

On September 26, 1905, Judge Bradford announced his decision. He found the "atmospheric contamination caused by the fish factories" unhealthy, and he ordered that the processing plants should use deodorizers, disinfectants and other methods to reduce the odors that emanated from the processing plants.

By the time this order went into effect, the usefulness of the Marine Hospital and quarantine station had begun to decline. The facility was closed shortly after World War I. The menhaden plants continued to flourish for several decades, until overfishing forced them out of business. The fish factories, marine hospital and the buildings of the quarantine station were all demolished, and there is not a hint of the odor from *United States v. Luce et al.*, "the Case of the Stinking Fish."

## I'D RATHER GO TO PRISON

"If it weren't for the disgrace it would bring on my family," a sea captain once said of serving aboard a lightship, "I'd rather go to prison." In 1892, lightship LV-46 was anchored east of Cape Henlopen to warn mariners of the dangerous Overfalls Shoals, and for nearly the next seven decades, a lightship with the name *Overfalls* painted in large white letters on each side of its bright red hull maintained this station three and a half miles east of Cape Henlopen.

Typically, lightships were a little more than one hundred feet long and twenty-five feet wide with a high freeboard that helped them withstand the waves of the Atlantic. In 1892, the *Overfalls* was a two-masted schooner that carried two larger lanterns, each having eight oil-burning lanterns. In addition, the *Overfalls* had a twelve-inch steam whistle and a hand-operated thousand-pound bell that could send warning signals when the waters around Cape Henlopen were encased in fog. The lightship was held in place by a

Tethered in place, the lightship *Overfalls* (LV-69) rides out the heavy waves. *Courtesy of the Delaware Public Archives.*

heavy chain that that was connected to a 6,500-pound mushroom anchor, shaped like an inverted saucer. Tethered in place, the pudgy lightship rolled incessantly with the waves so that "she washed her own decks." Life on a lightship was a combination of the boredom of solitary confinement and the misery of *mal de mer*.

Anchored near the mouth of Delaware Bay, the crew of the lightship *Overfalls* could only watch as a steady parade of sleek new steamers, graceful sailing ships and a host of smaller crafts made their way past Cape Henlopen. As these vessels plowed through the waves for some distant port, the stationary *Overfalls* sat placidly on the water as the days, weeks and months passed by.

Although under normal conditions, the *Overfalls* was anchored securely in place, an especially frigid winter in 1899 produced ice that swept the lightship temporarily off station. Two years later, the crew of the stationary *Overfalls* could only watch as another vessel approached and collided with the vessel. After the accident, the LV-46 was replaced by the newer LV-69 on the *Overfalls* station. The new *Overfalls* was powered by steam and had a cluster of three electric lens lanterns that were permanently mounted on each of the vessel's two masts.

During the early years of the twentieth century, the crew of the *Overfalls* saw more and larger steamships cruising past Cape Henlopen. Some of these vessels were equipped with wireless telegraphs that captains used to determine their locations with the help of a series of wireless stations, including one on Cape Henlopen that the U.S. Navy built along the East

Coast. In addition to the modern merchant vessels that steamed by the lightship, when the United States entered World War I in 1917, the crew of the *Overfalls* had a ringside seat to observe a small fleet of minelayers, minesweepers and submarine chasers descending upon the waters around Cape Henlopen.

The men on the *Overfalls*, however, were unable to spot the German submarine that arrived in the spring of 1918. On June 3, Captain H.H. Bennett of the tanker *Herbert L. Pratt* was bound for Philadelphia with a load of Mexican crude oil when the ship reached a point halfway between Rehoboth Beach and Lewes. Sailing nearby was the tanker *Arco*, which was not fully loaded, riding high in the water. As the *Herbert L. Pratt* steamed toward the *Overfalls*, Bennet heard a slight explosion, and at first, he thought that he had struck something submerged.

The *Herbert L. Pratt* may have been bumping over a sandbar, but Bennett believed his ship was severely damaged. He attempted to race past the *Overfalls* to the safety of the breakwater. After fifteen minutes, the *Pratt*'s engines stopped running, and the bow of the ship began to fill with water. Bennett immediately ordered all hands into the lifeboats. Fortunately, the pilot boat *Philadelphia* arrived on the scene, took aboard the men from the sinking tanker and transported them to Lewes. As the men were being rescued, Captain Bennett reported, "I saw the wake of what appeared to be a submarine approximately a thousand feet from starboard. This wake, I should say, was about two miles from where my vessel, the *Herbert L. Pratt*, was struck."

The report of a submarine caused consternation among the navy patrol boats that swarmed near the *Overfalls* as they hunted for the enemy ship. The captain of the tanker *Arco* believed that it was under attack as his ship hurriedly steamed past the lightship in a desperate effort to reach the safety of the breakwater. In the best tradition of jingoistic journalism, the *New York Times* reported, "He ran a gauntlet of shellfire, but managed to keep out of range till well inside the barrier, where the submarine would not follow."

The "gauntlet of shellfire" was imaginary; but the report that a German U-boat was off Cape Henlopen sent a small flotilla of patrol boats scurrying in pursuit of the phantom submarine. The *New York Times* breathlessly reported:

> *When they had reached a point seven miles off the coast they began firing violently, and it was believed by seafaring men here that they had picked up the trail of one of the U-boats. The firing continued until the scout ships went over the horizon…Tonight the waters surrounding the southern end*

*of New Jersey and the Delaware shore are swarming with chasers to give
battle to the Hun.*

The firing of the patrol boats rattled windows in Lewes and provided an
exciting diversion for the crew of the *Overfalls*, but the *Herbert L. Pratt* had
not been hit by a torpedo. The explosion was caused by a submerged mine,
which had been planted by a German submarine days earlier. Farther down
the coast off Fenwick Island, mines sunk the cargo ship *Saetia* and severely
damaged the battleship *Minnesota*.

When World War I ended in 1918, the crew of the *Overfalls* continued to
have a front-row seat to fiery events. On January 1, 1925, the liner *Mohawk*,
commanded by Captain James Staples, with over two hundred passengers
aboard, caught fire along the New Jersey coast. The fire resisted all efforts
by the crew of the *Mohawk* to extinguish it, and the fire worsened when the
flames reached several of the cars stored in the ship's hold. As clouds of black
smoke billowed through the ship, two tugs, the *Mars* and the *Kaleen*, steamed
out of Lewes Harbor to help. The Coast Guard cutter *Kickapoo*, stationed at
Cape May, also sailed into the storm to assist the burning ship. Anchored in
place, the crew of the *Overfalls* could only watch the drama unfold.

As Captain Staples steamed full speed ahead, those on board the *Mohawk*
remained surprisingly calm. George Scott, one of the passengers, later
recalled, "The smoke came up a bit and we assembled in the dining room
and waited. Some put on life-belts. Frightened? No, but many were seasick
[from] the way the ship was pitching."

Captain Staples passed between the lightship *Overfalls* and Cape May
as he turned the *Mohawk* into Delaware Bay. When the burning ship had
steamed ten miles into the bay, the *Mohawk* listed sharply to starboard
and tossed many of the passengers off their feet. The list prevented the
*Mohawk* from launching its lifeboats; but the Coast Guard cutter *Kickapoo*
and the tugs *Kaleen* and *Mars* arrived to assist the passengers trapped
aboard the burning vessel.

Although the seas were cold and choppy, all 290 of the *Mohawk*'s
passengers and crew were rescued and ferried to Lewes. Once ashore, the
survivors were taken to a special train that took them to Wilmington, where
some transferred to trains for New York, and others boarded trains that were
bound for Jacksonville, Florida, their original destination.

Later that year, an SOS was sent by another passenger ship, *Lenape*. In an
eerie repeat of the *Mohawk* fire, on November 17, 1925, *Lenape*, commanded
by Captain Charles Devereux, with over three hundred passengers on board,

also caught fire off the New Jersey coast. The ship's radio operator tapped out the message, "On fire eight miles southeast of east Five Fathom light, heading for Delaware breakwater."

While two Coast Guard cutters raced to rendezvous with the burning liner near the Overfalls Shoals, seventy-six-year old pilot Robert C. Chambers assembled the crewmen aboard the pilot boat *Philadelphia* and headed out to meet the burning liner. Instead of meeting near the shoals, the *Lenape* turned and steamed into the bay. As the pilot boat *Philadelphia* steamed alongside the *Lenape*, fire and smoke were belching from the ship, and cries could be heard: "For God's sake, save us!"

A small skiff carried veteran pilot Charles S. Morris to the *Lenape*, and he convinced Devereux to guide the *Lenape* to just beyond Lewes, where it could be run aground broadside to the wind. When the steamer came to a halt, the *Lenape*'s lifeboats began to drop over the ship's sides as fast as the davits could be operated. In addition, several small crafts that had been following the burning vessel for several miles immediately dashed for the *Lenape*. With a strong wind whipping the flames over the liner's stern, passengers climbed over the sides of the burning vessel and slid down ropes into the water.

As rescuers plucked survivors from the water, they were delivered to the *Philadelphia*, which had become a de facto hospital ship. Unfortunately, one of the passengers, sixty-year-old Robert Leverton, was waiting to be evacuated from the ship when flames burst through the deck. The panic-stricken Leverton grabbed a rope and jumped overboard. The rope slammed Leverton back into the ship, and he fell twenty-five feet into the water. His body was found by a fisherman hours later. All other passengers and crewmen were saved. Robert Orr, son of the surgeon at the Marine Hospital, recalled, "It was an awesome experience to watch from shore at night—the blazing ship moving in the Bay."

Aboard the *Philadelphia*, Chambers was in good humor as he ferried a crowd of survivors to Lewes. Knowing that the cold and frightened passengers from the *Lenape* would want a warm drink, Chambers quipped, "I didn't know I was going to have such a big party, so haven't much coffee, but if each of you will share his cup with another, each can have some."

The two fiery ship disasters lit up the Lewes night sky, but it was daytime when a small boat carrying a group of government commissioners sat quietly south of the Overfalls Shoals about to change the landscape of Cape Henlopen forever. The commissioners had been charged with finding a way to save the Cape Henlopen Lighthouse, and around noon, the commissioners decided to have lunch. When the Cape Henlopen

Lighthouse was constructed in the 1760s, it had stood on a high dune about a quarter mile from the surf, but within a few decades of its construction, people began to notice that dune on which the lighthouse stood was slowly eroding away. Some observers estimated that the dunes of Cape Henlopen were migrating westward at a rate of thirty to fifty feet a year. Some contended that the construction of the Delaware Breakwater caused a change in the ocean currents, which began to rob sand from the dune on which the lighthouse stood. Others believed that livestock that grazed near the lighthouse was killing the grasses that held the sand in place. Whatever

The windblown sand of Cape Henlopen piled up around the lighthouse. *Courtesy of the Delaware Public Archives.*

The rubble of the Cape Henlopen Lighthouse was strewn across the dune after it collapsed. *Courtesy of the Delaware Public Archives.*

the cause, the sands of Cape Henlopen continued to erode, and in 1926, the lighthouse stood on the edge of a sandy precipice. On April 13, while the commissioners who were studying ways to save the venerable old beacon were having lunch, the Cape Henlopen Lighthouse toppled onto the beach.

While residents of Lewes and Rehoboth Beach rushed to collect souvenirs from the lighthouse rubble, there were those who were pleased that one more coastal light had been extinguished. In 1919, the passage of the Eighteenth Amendment to the Constitution ushered in the prohibition of alcoholic beverages throughout the United States. Some residents of southern Delaware failed to see the wisdom of the forced abstention from alcohol, and many collaborated with the rumrunners who brought bootleg booze into the United States. Often, the illegal alcohol was brought from Canada in a mother ship to international waters off Cape Henlopen, where it would be loaded onto fast, smaller vessels for the final run into the bay. Other times, larger bootlegger boats would make the delivery without interruption. The *Correllis* was such a vessel. On November 16, 1931, the bootleggers aboard the rumrunner detested any light that would expose their position, and they steered clear of the lightship *Overfalls* as it sailed into Delaware Bay.

The *Correllis* turned toward shore near Slaughter Beach, and as the vessel slowed to a halt, the crew tossed cases of illegal alcohol overboard. The

Docked under the cannons of Memorial Park, these two bootlegger boats did not escape the authorities. *Courtesy of the Delaware Public Archives.*

containers of bootleg liquor were encased in weighted bags that quickly slipped below the surface. As the last four cases were dropped into water, a Coast Guard patrol boat arrived, and the bootleggers jumped overboard and waded ashore.

The Coast Guard seized two of the bootleggers and the abandoned *Correllis*, which could carry about ten thousand containers of bootleg whiskey, and before the government agents could fish the jettisoned alcohol out of the Delaware Bay, a crowd of local residents arrived on the beach armed with oyster and clam rakes to retrieve the sunken booze. Some people waded into the water until they hit the alcohol containers with their feet. After fifty cases of illegal moonshine had been retrieved, the Coast Guard put an end to the underwater scavenger hunt by firing shots over the heads of nimble-toed waders, setting off a brief mêlée.

Once the freelance foraging had been stopped, the government agents continued to retrieve the containers of bootleg alcohol. After dredging the bay waters all night, the recovered liquor was placed on trucks and sent to Wilmington, where it was turned over to the collector of customs. The two captured bootleggers were released on the grounds that they did not have any illegal alcohol with them when they were seized. The *Correllis* was taken to Lewes, where it was docked at the Lewes Town Wharf.

On January 5, 1932, several men were pumping the rumrunner's oily bilge water into the Lewes and Rehoboth Canal. When someone tossed a lit cigarette onto the oil slick that covered the water around the *Correllis*, the canal burst into flames. For a short time, the entire section of the canal was ablaze with flames that reached as high as the rooftops of nearby buildings. Those aboard the *Correllis* scurried ashore to escape the flames. Fortunately, Coast Guard personnel was able to extinguish the fire before anyone was hurt, but several vessels in the canal were damaged. The career of the rumrunner *Correllis*, however, was over.

It is impossible to tell how much illegal alcohol landed on the shores of Sussex County during Prohibition. Most of the time, the bootleggers arrived off the coast, unloaded their cargo and disappeared without a trace. When Prohibition ended, however, the crew of the *Overfalls* had one less thing to watch for to ease the monotony of their voyage to nowhere.

# DOG TAGS OF 1943

"There shall be built at Lewes a small building," stated the committee planning the tercentenary of the Dutch landing at Swanendael, "which shall represent as faithfully as possible the type of architecture of the town hall of Horn." Adopting an alternate spelling of the first European settlement in Delaware, the completion of the Zwaanendael Museum provided a distinctive landmark in the center of town that reminded residents and visitors of the Dutch origins of Lewes.

For a few weeks, the celebration of the town's beginnings helped to overshadow the gloomy economy. The Roaring Twenties had ended with a bang when the stock market crashed in 1929 and the Great Depression began. A month after President Franklin Roosevelt was inaugurated in 1933, Congress authorized the Civilian Conservation Corps. Several weeks later, work on CCC Camp 1224 began south of Lewes near the Savannah Road railroad crossing.

The CCC camps consisted of barracks, a medical office, a mess hall, officers' quarters, a recreation room and a warehouse. The camps were staffed by army officers, who used their military experience to organize and control the thousands of young men who joined the CCC. When the enlistees reported for duty, they were divided into companies of fifty men. After the men were issued ill-fitting army uniforms, they settled into a daily

The Zwaanendael Museum with its ornamented gable and carved stonework is an adaptation of the old town hall in Hoorn Holland. *Courtesy of the Delaware Public Archives.*

On this aerial photo of Lewes, the site of the CCC camp is at the lower center. *Courtesy of the Delaware Public Archives.*

Members of the CCC camp celebrate the history of Lewes dressed, not too accurately, as representative eras in the town's past for the 1936 homecoming parade. *Courtesy of the Delaware Public Archives.*

routine of constructing park shelters and picnic tables and digging miles of ditches to drain marshes to control the mosquito population.

In their spare time, members of the CCC camps organized orchestras, baseball teams and boxing squads. At the Lewes CCC camp, the men established a theatrical group that they named the "Strolling Marionettes," and they presented a series of three short plays. One of the most original pieces presented by the CCC theatrical troop was *Lust for Treasure*, which was billed, "The local story of the treasure ship *De Braak* forms the nucleus for this romantic drama in three acts."

Lewes remained mired in the Great Depression throughout the 1930s, and each year, the town's merchants pooled their resources to attract out-of-town buyers. Store owners were encouraged to decorate for the holidays, and a lottery was funded to award prizes to shoppers who patronized their stores. In the early twentieth century, the dynamos that generated the power for the town's early electric lights needed constant servicing. When it appeared that the system needed to be shut down, the electric company would signal the impending blackout by several short winks of dim power. When the town's residents saw their lights fade briefly, they knew it was time to revert to the traditional candles and oil lamps. By the 1930s, improvements to the town's electric generating system made electric lights more dependable, and to ensure a spectacular display of lights during the Christmas season, the board of public works gave customers a reduced rate during December and offered prizes for the best display.

By 1938, the deteriorating situation in Europe convinced the U.S. government to upgrade the defenses at the mouth of the Delaware Bay. Land was purchased on Cape Henlopen, and in 1940, several detachments of coast artillery batteries erected a small tent city on the dunes. Never designed to be permanent, the tents housed troops who waited for months for the temporary shelters to be replaced by lasting facilities and were named "Fort Miles" in honor of Nelson A. Miles, a Civil War general who served in the army for more than half a century.

When it was completed, Fort Miles contained several batteries of artillery that sat behind a concrete embankment covered with sand on the seaward side so that gun emplacements blended into the dune line. The sixteen-inch guns at Fort Miles were capable of firing a one-ton shell over twenty-five miles, and the batteries at Cape Henlopen needed spotters to report on the effectiveness of each shot. To house the spotters, a series of concrete towers was built along the beach. In addition, the gun batteries, spotting towers, barracks, administrative building, post chapel, gymnasium and a theater that also served as a dance hall were constructed at Fort Miles.

While work was proceeding on the fort on Cape Henlopen, the United States established the Aircraft Warning Service (AWS) to search the skies for enemy aircraft. Several Lewes women were among the spotting observers who were admonished, "Don't delay your report to get the exact number. Try

Tents that served as temporary quarters while Fort Miles was being constructed. *Courtesy of the Delaware Public Archives.*

to count the airplanes. If you can't count them—give your best estimate." The volunteers phoned sightings to a filter center run by the army air force, staffed by both military and civilian volunteer workers.

December 7, 1941, was a Sunday, and after church, families spent the day quietly, some listening to the radio. As they listened, the regular programming was interrupted by the news that the Japanese had attacked the American fleet at Pearl Harbor, Hawaii, and the United States was plunged into World War II. The next day, Mayor Thomas H. Carpenter of Lewes convened a meeting of civic leaders to organize the area's defense efforts. In the event that the town was attacked directly, first aid stations were to be established on the outskirts of Lewes so that Beebe Hospital would not be swamped. Plans were also developed for an automobile corps that would be used to

With the town and the fish plants in the background, the white buildings of Fort Miles sit back from the beach. *Courtesy of the Delaware Public Archives.*

evacuate schoolchildren. Eventually, buses and trucks were registered with the evacuation division of the Lewes Council of Defense, and evacuation officers visited households to give instructions on evacuation procedures to ensure that each person in Lewes had transportation in the event of a direct attack on the town.

In January 1942, Lewes residents drew darkening shades, streetlights were turned off and all vehicles came to a halt and extinguished their headlights in a test of the area's blackout procedures. Newly appointed air-raid wardens, assisted by members of the police and fire departments, observed the effectiveness of the blackout, which was deemed a success.

On the other side of the Atlantic Ocean, Admiral Karl Doenitz, the commander of the German submarine fleet, launched "Operation *Paukenschlag*" (Operation Drumroll), and in the middle of December 1941, five German U-boats sailed with orders to take up station between Cape Hatteras and the mouth of the St. Lawrence River. On Tuesday, January 27, 1942, the tanker *Francis Powell* was cruising northward along the coast toward Cape Henlopen. As the tanker pushed its way through the cold Atlantic waves, a German U-boat fired a single torpedo, which struck the *Francis Powell* in the port side with a devastating explosion that crippled the tanker. Water flooded into the vessel, which began to settle quickly, and the tanker disappeared beneath the waves. The crewmen made a frantic effort to lower the lifeboats as they abandoned the ship. Most of the crewmen of the American tanker had been asleep when the German torpedo exploded, and one of the crewmen sarcastically commented, "Well, they might have waited until we had breakfast."

When the sun came up, the men in the lifeboats were spotted by the Coast Guard cutter *W.C. Fairbanks*. After the men were picked up, the *W.C. Fairbanks* headed for Lewes. Reverend Nelson Rightmyer, rector of St. Peter's Episcopal Church and chairman of the Lewes branch of the Red Cross, was alerted by radio of the approach of the rescued sailors. He called for volunteers to collect blankets and prepare food and coffee for the rescued sailors. In addition, cots for the survivors were set up in the basement of the Lewes Coast Guard station. After the sailors arrived, they were given a hearty meal, and most of them enjoyed a warm and dry night's sleep. Three of the most seriously injured survivors were taken to Beebe Hospital. Except for those who were hospitalized, the sailors were transported to Philadelphia the next day.

The arrival of the survivors from the *Francis Powell* was a grim sign that Operation *Paukenschlag* had begun. For the rest of the winter, Lewes residents stood prepared to assist American seaman from ships that had been attacked along the coast. On February 2, 1942, the tanker *W.L. Steed* was torpedoed about one hundred miles from the coast. Two days later, German submarines sank the freighter *San Gil* and the tanker *Indian Arrow*. On February 28, two enemy torpedoes hit the destroyer *Jacob Jones*, named for the former resident of the Rhys Holt House, and it sank in less than an hour. During that dark winter, more than two hundred crewmen from thirteen torpedoed ships were rescued and brought into Lewes.

By the end of 1942, the institution of the convoy system and aerial surveillance of coastal waters greatly reduced the threat of U-boat attacks, and residents of Lewes focused their attention to winning the war at home. When the war began, panic-buying helped create an immediate shortage of sugar, and within a month, stores began to limit shoppers to two pounds per purchase. In May 1942, rationing officially began when all residents of Lewes were required to register for a book of ration coupons. Sugar, coffee and shoes were among the first items to be rationed, and they could not be bought without the proper coupons. Gasoline and tires were also strictly rationed, but fortunately, Lewes was a geographically compact town, where many residents walked to shopping, church and work.

In addition to rationing vital materials, each Saturday, town residents placed their old pots, pans, tools and other metal goods on the curb, where they were picked up so that the metal could be reused to fight the war. Caught up in the patriotic spirit of the campaign, one young coastal resident later confessed that he had taken several pots and pans from his mother's kitchen to donate to the drive. As volunteers scoured Lewes in search of items that could be recycled for the war effort, some people suggested that the cannons that lined Memorial Park contained a great deal of usable iron. When J. Orton Marshall, the treasurer of the town board of commissioners, learned that these reminders of the British attack during the War of 1812 seemed destined for the scrap drive, he commented, "These old guns are part of our town, and we'd hate to lose them; but we feel all of the scrap sources should be depleted." Fortunately, vigorous efforts to find other sources of scrap metal saved the large guns of Memorial Park from destruction, but that was not the case with the antique fire equipment. The two copper tanks that had been the first pieces of firefighting equipment of the Lewes Fire Company fell victim to the scrap drive.

As Lewes settled into a routine of collecting old metal goods, rubber products, cooking fats, rags and paper for the war effort, residents enjoyed a night of entertainment at Fort Miles. In 1943, the Fort Miles Players, composed of soldiers stationed at the facility, conceived, wrote and produced the musical show *Dog Tags of 1943*. After several preview shows at Rehoboth Beach and Georgetown, the first official performance was given at the Fort Miles Post Theatre on March 22 before invited civilian guests. *Dog Tags of 1943* was performed in vaudeville fashion with a series of skits, scenes and songs with original music, lyrics and gags written by the soldiers. The *Delaware Coast News* reported, "Corporal David E. Fitzgibbons, who directed 'Dog Tags of 1943', contributed some excellent dance routines, holding the audience spellbound with some tricky steps in two solo numbers. The talented dancer was heralded as the 'Fred Astaire of Fort Miles.'" The female roles were played by male soldiers, and a highlight of the show was a trio of the Fort Miles Players—Private Craig Edwards, Private Paul Millman and Corporal Charlie Lewis—singing "Why Did I Join the WAACS." Although the three men appeared in uniforms of the Women's Army Auxiliary Corps, their army boots and less-than-flattering wigs belied the report of the *Delaware Coast News* that the performers were "elaborately costumed."

In June 1942, German submarines landed two groups of enemy agents on American beaches near Jacksonville, Florida, and at Amagansett, Long Island. All eight saboteurs were quickly arrested, but the fact that two groups of enemy agents had been able to reach shore unchallenged demonstrated a major flaw in America's coastal defenses. In Delaware, the Coast Guard instituted routine mounted patrols of the beaches south of Cape Henlopen.

*Left to right:* Private Craig Edwards, Private Paul Millman and Corporal Charlie Lewis as WAACs in *Dog Tags of 1943. Courtesy of the Delaware Public Archives.*

In spite of the diligent patrols by the Coast Guard, in July 1943, Captain Justus B. Naylor stumbled onto a suspicious character in the basement of one of the buildings at Fort Miles. On July 25, the *New York Times* reported, "What appeared to be a 'very dead' dog was found on the basement floor of the fort's Surf club early this week by the post engineering office." The dog, emaciated and covered with oil and salt water, was alive but would not take food from anyone except Captain Naylor and snarled at everyone else. The animal, a male Gordon setter, wore a heavy leather collar with no identification, and the *Times* speculated, "It is known that the Nazi army specializes in the training of Gordon setters. There are various surmises about the dog here. One is that it is refugee from a sunken submarine, another that it was set ashore as a saboteur."

As far as is known, the mystery of the suspected German agent was never solved, but in 1944, German soldiers began to appear in and around Lewes. With so many people serving in the armed forces, workers were in short supply. In 1943, the lack of the usual migrant farm workers threatened the harvest of the bean crop and Sussex County farmers turned to the military authorities at Fort Miles. According to the *New York Times*, "Today [July 31] motorcades set forth from Fort Miles with coast artillerymen and from inland camps with infantrymen. It is expected that the troops will harvest crops for the next fortnight."

Although people were urged to forgo vacations to assist with the labor shortage on the farms, it was apparent something needed to be done to ease the labor situation in southern Delaware. At the beginning of the war, Delaware had been declared part of the Eastern Defense Command, and the military authorities prohibited the housing of captured enemy soldiers anywhere in this area. In early 1944, however, the War Department decided that the problems caused by the labor shortage outweighed the threat posed by escaped POWs; and in 1944, several POW camps were established in southern Delaware, including one near Lewes on the site of the old CCC camp. Before the war ended, several thousand captured Germans "invaded" southern Delaware to help relieve the labor shortage. In addition to farm

With the American flag flying, the U.S. Navy takes possession of the U-858. *Courtesy of the Delaware Public Archives.*

work, some of these captured soldiers worked in the fish processing plants on Cape Henlopen.

The people of Lewes had gotten used to the sight of German POWs on their way to work by Tuesday, May 8, 1945, when the ringing of church bells announced the end of the war in Europe. Before the Nazis surrendered, however, a few of the remaining operational submarines, including U-858, which was commanded by Captain Thilo Bode, steamed toward the Atlantic Coast. American surveillance planes spotted the German submarine, and navy ships soon arrived and fired several depth charges. Sensing that resistance was futile, Bode brought the submarine to the surface, where American warships surrounded the U-boat, and the Germans surrendered.

The U-858 was taken to the Delaware Breakwater, and the German crew was transferred ashore and driven to Fort Miles. When they were assembled and searched at the fort, the young crew, some of whom appeared to be teenagers, stood stoically. The war was over, but many of the people of Lewes and the guards at Fort Miles remembered the early days of the conflict when victims of German U-boats were brought ashore to Lewes.

Three months after the defeat of Germany, the dropping of atomic bombs on Hiroshima and Nagasaki hastened the defeat of Japan. The news of the surrender of Japan touched off a raucous celebration in Lewes. Those who had not heard the news broadcast on the radio were alerted by wailing of the Lewes Fire Department sirens, and people poured into the streets for a spontaneous demonstration that lasted throughout the day.

Under guard, the German crew of the U-858 awaits processing at Fort Miles. *Courtesy of the Delaware Public Archives.*

When the formal surrender of Japan took place on the battleship *Missouri*, Ensign James Kelly of Lewes was there. The son of a Delaware River pilot, Kelly had been commissioned in June 1944, and after seeing action in Philippines, he became the the junior officer of the deck aboard the destroyer *Nicholas*, which rendezvoused with a Japanese destroyer carrying the emissaries to be transferred to the American destroyer. The *Nicholas* steamed out to the USS *Missouri*, where Ensign Kelly escorted the Japanese officials aboard the American battleship and watched as they signed the surrender documents. World War II was, at last, over.

## MANY POINTS OF INTEREST

During the late nineteenth century, Lewes attracted a respectable number of visitors, including the artist Howard Pyle, who wrote that Lewes possessed "many points of interest," but in the twentieth century, other more prominent but less perceptive visitors failed to appreciate the town's diversions. On Saturday, June 9, 1923, President Warren G. Harding's motorcade made its way from Wilmington to Delaware, making stops at Dover and Milford for the president to deliver a short speech. At one point, Harding commented, "I did not know until today that Delaware was the first state to subscribe to the Union. I guess you were so small that you thought it would not hurt to do the right thing. It was a good thing." It was late night before the motorcade rolled into Lewes, where a crowd waited patiently for the president's arrival. After thanking the people for waiting hours for him, Harding said that the day had been one of the longest and most pleasant days of his life. He then boarded the presidential yacht *Mayflower* for the cruise back to Washington.

Two decades later, another presidential yacht, the USS *Williamsburg*, with President Harry Truman aboard, arrived off Cape Henlopen on August 17, 1946, and anchored near the breakwater. Truman was on a vacation cruise from Rhode Island to Bermuda, and the *New York Times* reported, "Near sunset the *Williamsburg* dropped anchor just inside Cape Henlopen and like a small boy just out of school, Mr. Truman hurriedly changed from slacks and sport shirt into a new pair of swim trunks." The *Williamsburg* lowered its gangway, and the president and several aides descended and plunged into the waters off Cape Henlopen. After swimming for about fifteen minutes, the president returned to the *Williamsburg*. According to the ship's log, "At 1710, the swimming party, completely refreshed, returned aboard." Later that week, *Delaware Coast News* belatedly reported on the stealth swimmer: "Little did the residents of Lewes realize as they were enjoying their evening meals on Sunday…that the First Citizen of the USA, President Harry S. Truman, was swimming in the Delaware Breakwater, almost within sight of the town!"

Three years after President Truman's impromptu swim off Cape Henlopen, Russian visitors steamed through the mouth of Delaware Bay, as a dispute over access to Berlin had driven the United States and the Soviet Union to the edge of open combat. In June 1948, Joseph Stalin of the Soviet Union blockaded the roads to Berlin, and President Truman responded by initiating a massive airlift of supplies to the city. By September 1948, the airlift was carrying 4,500 tons of food and other supplies into the besieged city every day. Tension continued to mount throughout the winter, and on March 10, 1949, Soviet warships appeared off Cape Henlopen.

Around noon, word was received in Lewes that the Soviet cruiser *Murmansk* was approaching the bay, and a Coast Guard cutter led a small flotilla of boats seaward to intercept it. Aboard the *Murmansk*, the Soviet crew stood rigidly at attention as the cruiser began to reduce speed. The *Murmansk* dropped anchor about five miles north of Cape Henlopen, and as the *Delaware Coast News* noted, "An icy chill seemed to sweep from the decks of the man of war to the bobbing Coast Guard Cutter as it circled the craft. Not a Soviet sailor or officer waved. Not even the *Tass* correspondent, representative of the official Soviet News Agency, waved back to his comrades from Russia."

Aboard the *Murmansk*, the crew stood rigidly at attention as the Soviet military attaché, his assistant and a Lewes pilot boarded the vessel. During World War II, the United States had lent the Soviet Union fifteen American warships to help protect the shipping lanes from German U-boat attacks. One of these warships was the USS *Milwaukee*, which the Soviet Union renamed the *Murmansk*, and the Soviets had chosen this moment, while the Berlin airlift was in full swing, to return the warship to the United States. At 1:40 p.m., Captain Joseph U. Lademan Jr. of the U.S. Navy climbed aboard the *Murmansk*, where he signed a receipt for the cruiser. Less than an hour later, the Soviet flag was lowered as the band played the Soviet national anthem. Fifteen minutes later, the ship was officially back in the possession of the U.S. Navy.

During the next two and half hours, a tug ferried the Soviet sailors from the *Murmansk* to the transport *Molotov*. When the last Russian had left the ship, the return of the cruiser to America was completed. The

The transfer completed and its old name restored, the USS *Milwaukee* began its final voyage to Philadelphia. *Courtesy of the Lewes Historical Society.*

Russians had insisted that the transfer be conducted without any pomp or ceremony, and it was suspected that it was done in this manner so that the Soviet crew would not have to give a courtesy salute to the American flag.

Once they were aboard the cruiser, the American sailors quickly went to work stripping the vessel of any sign of its Russian use. The Stars and Stripes replaced the Russian flag, and the Soviet-style white waterline stripe was painted over. After the name *Murmansk* on the ship's stern was replaced with *Milwaukee*, the ship was ready to begin the short trip to Philadelphia, where the vessel was to be scrapped.

The return of the *Milwaukee* seemed indicate a pause in the politics of confrontation that marked the Cold War, and two months later, the Soviets lifted the blockade of Berlin. The Russian sailors aboard the cruiser were not allowed to go ashore, much less visit the historic sites of Lewes. As the *Delaware Coast News* noted, "For them, the coastline was the shore dimly seen."

Not all of the out-of-towners made transitory visits to Lewes. Otis Smith arrived in Lewes in 1938, when his family purchased the Harley Joseph fish-processing plant on the cape, and he began a program that transformed the menhaden fishing business. He had a small fleet of specially designed boats built. These steel-hulled vessels were equipped with electronic units that calmed the fish after they were corralled in the nets. Smith's boats were also equipped with pumps that removed the fish from the seine nets. When the boats reached Cape Henlopen, a vacuum helped unload the catch at the rendering plants. Smith also improved the processing techniques by using dryers that dramatically reduced the odors that had often surrounded the plants.

World War II temporarily slowed the progress of the menhaden industry, but during the war, small aircraft demonstrated the practicality of spotting German submarines from the air. After the war, Smith employed spotter planes to locate schools of menhaden and radio directions to Smith's fleet of two dozen boats. Smith had turned menhaden fishing into a finely tuned operation, and his success helped make Lewes the largest fish-landing port in the country. At its peak in 1956, 360 million pounds of fish were landed in Lewes. Smith had transformed the local fishing industry, but as his business prospered, the Lewes town government was spiraling toward bankruptcy.

In 1950, the town of Lewes was spending $9,000 more than it took in, and the town had accumulated $40,000 in debt. With an annual budget of less than $60,000 a year, there seemed to be no way to save the town from bankruptcy. But Smith had learned the history of Lewes well, and he decided to run for mayor. According to the *New York Times*, "Owner of the Fish Products Company, one of the world's largest menhaden processing plants in the world, Mr. Smith was the first 'outlander' to be Mayor in the 321-year history of Lewes, traditional home of the pilots who guide merchant vessels between Cape Henlopen and Philadelphia."

Mayor Otis Smith, *second from left*, was an advocate for Lewes and its history. *Courtesy of the Delaware Public Archives.*

After Smith settled into office, he announced that he was suing the state of Delaware. According to the *New York Times*:

> *Soon after taking office Mayor Smith sued the State of Delaware for $61,644 that it had received from the Federal Government for 1,010 acres of land on Cape Henlopen. He contended that the money belonged to Lewes because the tract, now the site of the Fort Miles Artillery Post was part of the original grant of land placed in trust by William Penn in 1682 for the benefit of "the inhabitants of Lewes."*

Smith won the suit, and the town had enough money to wipe out the debt, saving the town from bankruptcy. He was so successful that he was reelected without opposition. In addition to serving as mayor of Lewes for eighteen years, Smith was a major benefactor to Lewes and Sussex County. He helped establish utility lines to Lewes Beach, he served on the board of Beebe Hospital and he helped establish the Marine Laboratories, the predecessor to the College of Marine Studies on Pilottown Road. Smith also worked with civil rights leaders to help ease the desegregation process in the 1950s and 1960s. Lewes fishermen, however, were so efficient that the menhaden population was quickly depleted. Following the peak catch of 1956, the menhaden population declined precipitously, and in 1966, the last processing plant was closed.

Of all the visitors to Lewes, some of the most powerful were the storms that periodically passed by the town. In October 1693, Lewes was still a small colonial village when the area was struck by a strong storm that battered the dunes and created new channels between the coastal bays and the ocean. A half century later, in 1749, Lewes had grown into a much larger town when a hurricane passed over Cape Henlopen, and several vessels that had taken refuge in Lewes Harbor were blown ashore. The storm eroded a channel across the neck of Cape Henlopen, and for a time, shallow draft boats could take a shortcut to the sea. In the nineteenth century, Lewes was buffeted by several strong hurricanes, and in 1888 and 1889, nor'easters battered Lewes, from which dozens of vessels were sunk or damaged.

During the first week of March 1962, two low-pressure systems combined off the coast to create a nor'easter of devastating proportions. The lumbering storm took several days to pass by the Delaware coast. During this time, the coastal resorts were pounded by wind, rain and an exceptionally high tide.

Viewed from the bridge over the canal, the flooding at Lewes Beach in 1962 is readily apparent. *Courtesy of the Delaware Public Archives.*

Although Lewes escaped relatively unscathed, there was a great deal of damage near the canal. *Courtesy of the Lewes Historical Society.*

The Rehoboth Beach boardwalk was destroyed, and half of the Henlopen Hotel was washed into the sea. In Lewes, there was extensive damage to the boats and wharves in the canal, but the bluff on which the town was built served Lewes well. Although there was extensive flooding at Lewes Beach, Lewes escaped relatively unscathed, and the storm left intact the town's "many points of interest."

## When You Go

The development on the beachfront at the cape has obliterated most signs of the quarantine station and the fish-processing plants. The wooden frame buildings of the quarantine station were dismantled without difficulty, but the fourteen-story silo built by Sea Coast Products was another matter. The rectangular silo was constructed with reinforced concrete walls up to

In this 1960 photo, the fish plants are at the upper center. *Courtesy of the Delaware Public Archives.*

eighteen inches thick. In addition, the interior walls were interconnected in a way that gave the building enormous strength and stability. In 1983, the empty building stood on valuable bayfront land that developers wanted for the Port Lewes townhouses. In March, the dynamiters attempted to level the structure, but when the charges ignited, the building tilted to one side and stayed stubbornly in place. For six weeks, the demolition team battled the building, which became known as the "Leaning Tower of Lewes." The tilting silo attracted scores of sightseers, but in May, another blast of three hundred pounds of explosives toppled the slanting silo onto its side, where it could be knocked into rubble and hauled away.

Advance lighted automated buoys and the development of high-tech navigation systems rendered the lightship *Overfalls* obsolete. In 1973, lightship LV-118 was renamed *Overfalls* and brought to Lewes. Currently, the vessel is moored near the boathouse of the Lewes Life-Saving Station next to Canalfront Park. The lightship is listed on the National Register of Historic Places, under the care of the *Overfalls* Maritime Museum Foundation. When super storm Sandy swept Lewes in 2013, the *Overfalls*, which had experienced far worse on the open sea, remained stoically in place.

The lightship *Overfalls* is now securely moored as a museum ship next to Canalfront Park. *Photo by Michael Morgan.*

The Atlantic Ocean seen from atop the Great Dune in Cape Henlopen State Park. *Photo by Michael Morgan.*

Cape Henlopen Lighthouse, which once helped guide mariners through the treacherous waters off Cape Henlopen, of course, is gone. After the beacon fell in 1926, coastal residents descended on the pile of rubble that had once been the lighthouse to scavenge for souvenirs. Those scraps of the tower that were not carted off were soon covered by the shifting sands, and the location of the lighthouse became a faded memory.

Reminders of the lighthouse, the fish-processing plants and the quarantine station have quickly faded from view, but over a half century since it became obsolete, the towers of Fort Miles remain on the Delaware sands. The bulk of the grounds of Fort Miles are now part of Cape Henlopen State Park, and the Fort Miles Historical Association has been working to restore gun emplacements, spotting towers

*Top*: The Fort Miles Historical Association has made great strides in restoring Fort Miles to its World War II appearance. *Photo by Michael Morgan.*

*Left*: At Cape Henlopen State Park, visitors can climb to the top of one of Fort Miles's spotting towers and get a commanding view of the coast. *Photo by Michael Morgan.*

A log cabin is just one building at the Lewes Historical Society's complex on Shipcarpenter Street. *Photo by Michael Morgan.*

and other structures to create a lasting memorial to the men and women who served at this installation.

In 1962, a small group of civic-minded citizens incorporated the Lewes Historical Society "to preserve what are left of the old houses in Lewes [and] to propose zoning laws which will add to the beauty of the town." The Burton-Ingram house was saved and moved to a newly acquired lot at the corner of Third and Shipcarpenter Streets, where it was joined by Thompson Country store, an early plank house and a blacksmith shop. The Cannonball House was purchased, and the society acquired a large number of paintings, books, furniture and other items. The society's holdings and programs continue to grow, featuring a variety of tours, a yearly journal and a strong Internet presence. With a town filled with so much history, the Lewes Historical Society has done excellent work to ensure that this history no longer remains hidden.

# BIBLIOGRAPHY

*Annual Report of the United States Life-Saving Service for the Fiscal Year Ending June 30, 1888.* Washington, D.C.: Government Printing Office, 1889.

Archdeacon, Herbert. "The Breakwaters." *Journal of the Lewes Historical Society* 3 (November, 2000).

Bates, Samuel. *History of Pennsylvania Volunteers, 1861–5.* Vol. 5. Harrisburg, PA: B. Singerly, State Printers, 1871.

Beach, John (Jack) W. *The Cape Henlopen Lighthouse.* Dover, DE: Henlopen Publishing Co., 1970.

Bellas, Henry Hobart, ed. *Personal Recollections of Captain Enoch Anderson.* Wilmington: Historical Society of Delaware, 1896.

Benson, Barbara E. "Delaware Goes to War." *Delaware History* 26, nos. 3–4, (Spring/Summer 1995–Fall/Winter 1995–96).

Booth, Iva Short, Martha Torbert Hudson and Paulette Bier Shaw. *Georgetown: From Crossroads to County Seat; A Bicentennial Look at Georgetown, Delaware.* Georgetown, DE: Georgetown Historical Society, 1990.

Brittingham, Hazel D. *Lantern on Lewes: Where the Past is Present.* Lewes, DE: Lewestown Publishers, 1998.

Cohen, William J. *Swanendael in New Netherland.* Wilmington, DE: Cedar Tree Books, 2004.

Conner, William H., and Leon deValinger Jr. *Delaware's Role in World War II.* Dover, DE: Public Archives Commission, 2003.

Constance J. Cooper. "Make It Do or Do Without: Delawareans and Rationing During World War II." *Delaware History* 26, nos. 3–4 (Spring/Summer 1995–Fall/Winter 1995–96).

Cox, S.S. "The Life Saving Service." *North American Review* 132, no. 294 (May 1881).

Dalleo, Peter T. "South of the Canal in the 1840s as Described in the *Blue Hen's Chicken.*" *Delaware History* 29, no. 2 (Fall/Winter 2000–01).

"Deposition of Helmanus Wiltbank and Others." *Historical Society of Pennsylvania.* 1454 Cadwalader Collection, Series III (Thomas) Box 31 F#3.

DiPaolo, E. Michael. "Protecting 'Old Lewes': History of the Lewes Historical Society." *Journal of the Lewes Historical Society* 14 (November 2011).

Doughty, Frances Albert. "Life at a Life-Saving Station." *Catholic World* 65, no. 388 (July 1897).

Franklin, H. Bruce. "The Most Important Fish in the Sea," *Discover* 22, no. 9 (September 2001).

Gentile, Gary. *Shipwrecks of Delaware and Maryland.* Philadelphia: Gary Gentile Productions, 1990.

George, Pam. *Shipwrecks of the Delaware Coast.* Charleston, SC: The History Press, 2010.

*German Submarine Activities on the Atlantic Coast of the United States and Canada.* Washington, D.C.: Government Printing Office, 1920.

Grunder, Betty. "Henry Brooke: Colonial Poet." *Journal of the Lewes Historical Society* 7 (November 2004).

———. "Mayor Otis H. Smith." *Journal of the Lewes Historical Society* 6 (November 2003).

———. "Up in Smoke." *Journal of the Lewes Historical Society* 11 (November 2008).

———. "The Wilson-Wiley Murder." *Journal of the Lewes Historical Society* 9 (November 2006).

Hancock, Harold B. *Delaware, Two Hundred Years Ago: 1780–1800.* Wilmington, DE: Mid-Atlantic Press, 1987.

———. "The Revolutionary War Diary of William Adair." *Delaware History* 13, no. 2 (April 1968).

———. "Thomas Robinson: Delaware's Most Prominent Loyalist." *Delaware History* 4, no. 1 (March 1950).

Hazard, Samuel, ed. *The Register of Pennsylvania.* Vol. 7, *January to July, 1831.* Philadelphia: William F. Geddes, printer, 1831.

Hickan, Homer H., Jr. *Torpedo Junction.* New York: Dell Publishing, 1989.

Holland, Randy J. *Delaware's Destiny Determined by Lewes.* Dover: Delaware Heritage Press, 2013.

Holl, Richard E. "Axis Prisoners of War in the Free State, 1943–1946." *Maryland Historical Magazine* 83 (Summer 1988).

Horle, Craig, ed. *Records of the Sussex County Delaware, 1677–1710.* Vols. 1–2. Philadelphia: University of Pennsylvania Press, 1991.

Ippolito, James C. "Quarantine Station." In *The Delaware Estuary: Rediscovering a Forgotten Resource.* Edited by Tracey L. Bryant and Jonathan R. Pennock. Newark: University of Delaware Sea Grant Program, 1992.

Jordan, Francis. *Aboriginal Fishing Stations on the Coast of the Middle Atlantic States.* Philadelphia: New Era Printing Company, 1906.

———. *The Remains of an Aboriginal Encampment at Rehoboth Delaware.* Philadelphia: Numismatic and Antiquarian Society of Philadelphia, 1880.

Keith, Charles P. *The Provincial Councilors of Pennsylvania.* Philadelphia: W.S. Sharp, 1883.

Kern, John R. "The Election Riots of 1787 in Sussex County, Delaware." *Delaware History* 22, no. 4 (Fall/Winter 1987).

Kobbe, Gustav. "Life on the South Shoal Lightship." *Century Magazine* 42, no. 4 (August 1891).

Kotowski, Bob. *Ablaze in Lewes Harbor: The Last Cruise of the SS* Lenape. Wilmington, DE: Cedar Tree Books, 2007.

Martin, Roger Allen. "The Wiley-Wilson Murder." *Delaware Lawyer* 1, no. 3 (Winter/Spring 1983).

Mills, Eric. *Chesapeake Rumrunners of the Roaring Twenties.* Centreville, MD: Tidewater Publishers, 2000.

Morgan, William. *Diary.* Microfilm, Stephen J. Betze Library, Delaware Technical Community College, Jack F. Owens Campus, Seaford, 1851.

*Naval Documents of the American Revolution.* Vols. 1–10. Washington, D.C.: Government Printing Office, 1969–96.

Orr, Robert Hunter. *A Small-Town Boyhood in the First State.* Denver, CO: Privately printed, 1999.

Paine, Ralph. *The Book of Buried Treasure.* London: William Hienemann, 1911.

Perry, Lyn. *Some Letters of and Concerning Major William Peery.* Strasburg, VA: Shenandoah Publishing House, 1935.

Pusey, Pennock. "History of Lewes, Delaware." In *Papers of the Historical Society of Delaware*. Vol. 38. Wilmington: Historical Society of Delaware, 1903.

Pyle, Howard. "A Peninsular Canaan." *Harper's Monthly* 59, no. 350 (July 1879).

Rau, Charles. *Prehistoric Fishing in Europe and North America*. Washington, D.C.: Smithsonian Institution, 1884.

*Register of Pennsylvania* 4, no. 25 (December 19, 1829).

Ritchie, Robert C. *Captain Kidd and the War against the Pirates*. New York: Barnes and Noble, 2006.

Scharf, J. Thomas. *History of Delaware*. Philadelphia: J.L. Richards and Co., 1888.

Sebold, Kimberly R. "The Delmarva Broiler Industry and World War II: A Case in Wartime Economy." *Delaware History* 25, no. 3 (Spring/Summer 1993).

Sellers, Edwin Jaquett. *Captain John Avery*. Philadelphia: J.P. Lippincott, 1897.

Shomette, Donald. *The Hunt for HMS* De Braak*: Legend and Legacy*. Durham, NC: Carolina Academic Press, 1993.

Shorto, Russell. *The Island at the Center of the World*. New York: Vintage Books, 2005.

Smith, John. *The Generall Historie of Virginia, New-England, and the Summer Isles*. Vol. 1. New York, 1907.

Spears, John R. "Sand-Waves at Henlopen and Hatteras." *Scribner's Magazine* 8 (July–December 1890).

Stacton, David. *The Bonapartes*. New York: Simon and Schuster, 1966.

Thompson, Joanne, and Judith Adkins Roberts. "The History of the Delaware River Pilots." In *One Hundred Year History of the Pilots' Association Bay and River Delaware, 1896–199*. Edited by Andrew Knopp. Wilmington: Delaware Heritage Press, 1996.

Trapani, Bob, Jr. *Delaware Lights: A History of the Lighthouses in the First State*. Charleston, SC: The History Press, 2007.

Trudeau, Andre. *Like Men of War*. Edison, NJ: Castle Books, 1998.

Turner, C.H.B., ed. *Daniel Rodney's Diary and Other Delaware Records*. Philadelphia: Allen, Lane and Scott, 1911.

————. *Some Records of Sussex County*. Philadelphia: Allen, Lane and Scott, 1909.

Ward, Christopher. *The Delaware Continentals*. Wilmington: Historical Society of Delaware, 1941.

Weslager, C.A. *A Brief Account of the Indians of Delaware*. Newark: University of Delaware, 1953.

————. *Delaware's Buried Past*. New Brunswick, NJ: Rutgers University Press, 1968.

————. "The Lenape Indians." In *The Delaware Estuary: Rediscovering a Forgotten Resource*. Edited by Tracey L. Bryant and Jonathan R. Pennock. Newark: University of Delaware Sea Grant Program, 1992.

————. *The Siconese Indians of Lewes, Delaware: A Historical Account of a "Great" Bayside Lenape Tribe*. Lewes, DE: Lewes Historical Society, 1991.

## NEWSPAPERS

*Delaware Coast News*
*Delaware Coast Press*
*Manufacture and Builder*
*New York Times*
*Salisbury Times*
*State News*

## NEWSPAPER ABSTRACTS

From www.newspaperabstracts.com.
*Baltimore Patriot*
*Baltimore Sun*
*Boston Journal*
*Chester Daily Times*
*Cincinnati Commercial Tribune*
*Connecticut Courant*
*Easton Star*
*Miami Herald*
*Missouri Courier*
*Philadelphia Inquirer*
*Public Ledge and Daily Transcript*
*Trenton Evening Times*
*Washington Post*

## ONLINE SOURCES

Afro-Anglicans Online. "Absalom Jones Biography." afroanglicans.org.

Archives of Maryland. "Proceedings of the Council of Maryland." Vols. 2, 15. www.mdarchives.state.md.us.

Callander, Bruce D. "The Ground Observer Corps." airforce-magazine. com 89, no. 2 (February 2006). www.airforce-magazine.com.

Dennis, W.A., G.A. Lanan and R.A. Dalrymple. "Chapter 75: Case Studies of Delaware's Tidal Inlets; Roosevelt and Indian River Inlets." journals. tdl.org/icce/index.php/icce/article/viewFile/3337/3005.

EyeWitnesstoHistory.com. "Yellow Fever Attacks Philadelphia, 1793." www. eyewitnesstohistory.com/yellowfever.htm.

Flint, Willard. "A History of U.S. Lightships." www.uscg.mil/history/ articles/Lightships.pdf.

History of St. George's AME Church. www.ourchurch.com/view/?pageID=291370.

Kelly, James. "A Full and True Discovery of All the Robberies, Pyracies, and other Notorious Actions of that Famous English Pyrate, Capt. James Kelly." www.galapagos.to/texts/KELLY.HTM.

"Log of the President's Vacation Cruise, August 16-Septemeber 2, 1946, USS *Weiss* (APD 135)." www.stevenlfletcher.com/weiss/weissstory.html.

McVae, Bridget Christine. "The Roosevelt Inlet Shipwreck: Identification, Analysis, and Historical Context." Master's theses, Texas A&M University, 2008. anthropology.tamu.edu/papers/McVae-MA2008.pdf.

*Overfalls* Maritime Museum Foundation. www.overfalls.org.

Truman Presidential Museum and Library. http://www.trumanlibrary.org/calendar/travel_log/textview.php?docid=cruise46.

# ABOUT THE AUTHOR

Michael Morgan has been writing freelance newspaper articles on the history of coastal Delaware for over three decades. He is the author of the Delaware Diary, which appears weekly in the *Delaware Coast Press*, and the Sussex Journal, which is a weekly feature of the *Wave*. Morgan has also published articles in the *America's Civil War*, the *Baltimore Sun*, *Chesapeake Bay Magazine*, *Civil War Times*, *Maryland Magazine*, *World War II Magazine* and other national publications. Morgan's look at history is marked by a lively, storytelling style that has made his writing and lectures popular. Michael Morgan is also the author of *Pirates and Patriots: Tales of the Delaware Coast, Rehoboth Beach: A History of Surf and Sand, Bethany Beach: A Brief History*, *Ocean City: Going Down the Ocean* and *Civil War Delaware: The First State Divided*.

Photo by Madelyn Morgan.

*Visit us at*
www.historypress.net
........................................................
*This title is also available as an e-book*